OFF THE
DEEP
END

OFF THE DEEP END

JERRY *and* BECKI FALWELL *and the* COLLAPSE *of an* EVANGELICAL DYNASTY

GIANCARLO GRANDA

with **MARK EBNER**

wm

WILLIAM MORROW

An Imprint of HarperCollinsPublishers

HarperCollins books may be purchased for educational, business, or sales promotional use. For information, please email the Special Markets Department at SPsales@harpercollins.com.

FIRST EDITION

Designed by Nancy Singer

Library of Congress Cataloging-in-Publication Data has been applied for.

ISBN 978-0-06-322734-7

22 23 24 25 26   LSC   10 9 8 7 6 5 4 3 2 1

You have not strengthened the weak or healed the sick or bound up the injured. You have not brought back the strays or searched for the lost. You have ruled them harshly and brutally.

—*Ezekiel 34:4 (New International Version)*

CONTENTS

Everything that follows is true. I've re-created scenes to the best of my ability. Where the dialogue isn't reproduced from documentary sources—texts, recordings, videotapes, news accounts—I've presented them as I remembered them, and have preserved their true essence. And I've got a wealth of texts, tapes, photos, emails, private interviews, secondary confirmations, and eyewitness testimony to back up my claims.

I'm not proud of everything I've done. But it's all a part of my story, so I'm trying to own it. I would have preferred to go about my life, free from drama and controversy. But this is my path, and so to the extent that my story is bigger than I am, I have tried to render it faithfully.

OFF THE DEEP END

THAT GUY

My name is Giancarlo Granda. Unfortunately, I am better known as "the pool boy," the one who embarked on an ill-considered affair with Becki Falwell, wife of Jerry Falwell Jr., the oldest son and namesake of the late founder of the Moral Majority, and the heir to his evangelical dynasty. I was twenty when it started, working at the fabled Fontainebleau Hotel in Miami, and I had never had a steady girlfriend.

That momentary lapse in judgment on a sunny day in March 2012 has now consumed a third of my thirty-odd years, or roughly my entire adult life. Moreover, it lit a long and winding fuse that has seen Falwell forced to resign as president of Liberty University in Lynchburg, Virginia, one of the largest evangelical universities in the world, a legacy position he inherited upon his father's death. Pending an independent audit, it may further expose any number of questionable financial dealings, real estate transactions, secret agreements, and instances of crony capitalism masterminded by Falwell over the course of his decade-and-a-half tenure. Along the way, I caught wind of others like me, who had stumbled into their web and were still buzzing around its edges. Except that unlike me, they didn't wind up a national punch line.

More importantly, my transgression has managed to shine a light on Liberty University as the private fiefdom of this charmed family—and a whole host of possibly unlawful actions only now coming to light—overseen by their handpicked board of rank apologists and moral relativists. Nowhere does this disparity between appearances and actions stand in starker relief than in how those private ethics and double standards I witnessed from inside the Falwells' bubble, the couple's wildly inappropriate and reckless sexual behavior, inflamed by a regal sense of entitlement, have given rise to Liberty's privileged, predatory culture, one that eventually would engender an epidemic of sexual violence. That so many among this often naive and sheltered student body were sent there by overprotective parents terrified of the secular world makes it all the more tragic and predictable. Liberty and the worldview it embraced turned out to be a con in so many ways.

Falwell Jr.'s 2016 endorsement of Donald J. Trump helped deliver Trump the evangelical vote, securing him both the Republican nomination and the presidency (just as the senior Falwell's Moral Majority facilitated the election of Ronald Reagan in 1980). That endorsement was allegedly brokered by Trump's private fixer Michael Cohen (calling in a favor, as he calls it in *Disloyal*, the book he wrote in prison) after he claimed to have made the details of my affair—and the graphic photos that would have made denying it pointless—quietly go away. So my simple youthful indiscretion, which has caused me embarrassment and regret—not to mention a very real fear for my own safety—may also have played a not insignificant role in making a person like Trump president.

My choices ultimately pitched me into a rarefied world of political influence and financial brinksmanship. At one point I was threatened by an armed individual and told, "Keep your mouth shut." Exactly the ultimatum I'm violating as I write this. Even that epithet "pool boy" became part of an orchestrated campaign to ridicule me and diminish my standing in the eyes of the media and their scandal-addled audience. I am shackled to the name and the sordid tale it conjures—an albatross around my neck. Forever.

What follows is my story—at least as much of it as I can see from where I'm standing—and I'm grateful for the opportunity to share it. I hope by the end of it, you'll see me less as a pool boy and more as a flawed human who is trying to reclaim his identity and his dignity. Perhaps, too, this will serve as a cautionary tale for those of us who fall prey to the powerful and the influential. Either way, it is, above all, the truth.

CHAPTER 2

MIAMI BLUES

Miami is America's fabled "Magic City," where the normal high school preoccupations of sex, money, ambition, status, and assimilation are shared by the population at large, and perpetually at a high boil. "Home of the newly wed and the nearly dead" they say, and I saw those sorts of extremes built into every aspect of the town.

I am the proud son of immigrants: a Cuban father from a semi-prominent middle-class family who fled Havana and the revolution in 1960, whose grandfather (my great-grandfather) was an engineer and later the minister of public works under Carlos Prío Socarrás before the military coup that brought Batista to power. He eventually amassed a fortune in Cuban real estate, all of which was seized by Castro. Like every expatriate he knew, he went to his grave believing he would one day return to Havana and reclaim his empire.

Similarly, my mother emigrated from Mexico City, where her uncle (my godfather) owned a bakery and later his own multi-unit apartment building. In addition, my godmother's husband is an architect and developer of gated communities, and both my sister and I have been interested in real estate development from an early age. My parents met in Miami in 1980, shortly after my mother's arrival, where my father managed a chain of beeper stores, which were extremely popular, this being the era of *Miami Vice*. My sister was born in 1984, and I came along seven years later. We were close, and remain so today. She currently works in the high-end residential real estate industry.

By the time I reached high school, I had an affinity for economics and its real-world application, excelling in my high school accounting class. My parents both encouraged my interest in real estate, and when we would visit Mexico City, my godfather always went out of his way to walk me through the business. I was also a fan of Donald Trump, then considered a real estate maverick on the strength of the persona he put forth in *The Art of the Deal*. I believed the hype, was predictably conservative in my politics (being the son of a Cuban exile), and secretly imagined I might one day fulfill my own dream of becoming a real estate mogul.

I grew up middle class in Westchester, a working-class Cuban neighborhood. The Cuban exile community is like any other tribe that has been forced out of its homeland: its descendants are resilient members of a diaspora, always preoccupied with a place that no longer exists, save for the burnished tales handed down over time that evolve as they drift from their original source. Cubans represent over half the population of Miami, and as much as 80 percent of enclaves like Westchester and Hialeah. Conservative politicians can exploit this generational trauma to consolidate power and lock in a reliable voting bloc, so long as they celebrate personal liberty, limited government, and never bend the knee to Castro. This in turn stokes expatriate grievances and can inflate the expat community's sense of self-worth. Mix that with a genetic disposition toward prodigious energy and self-motivation, and you've got a force to be reckoned with. Cubans in Miami exert an outsize influence in local politics, the construction trades, and real estate in general.

Although I attended Catholic high school, I was never particularly religious, although the trappings were never far away. My mother was the religious one in the family; she eventually became a born-again Christian and went a little off the deep end herself—joining a storefront evangelical church that was eventually revealed as a racket. And she was a regular viewer of the Christian Broadcasting Network, which includes among its stable of talent Jonathan Falwell, Jerry Jr.'s brother and chief pastor of Thomas Road Baptist Church, founded by his father, and just down the road from Liberty University in Lynchburg, Virginia.

I get along well with both my parents. They have always been there for me, and are model parents in many ways, but my dad lacked the emotional capacity to connect with me. There was always something missing at the core of our relationship. It may have closed me off to other people, as well as the social possibilities that high school had to offer.

As this was Miami I had a lot of friends from wealthy families, and so from an early age I was comfortable around money and the people who had it. A lot of my friends' parents were successful real estate developers, hotel owners, lawyers, or just mysteriously well off. After the austerity of the sixties and seventies, where people with money often didn't advertise it, Miami in the eighties was all about conspicuous consumption, the more ostentatious the better. By the same token, rubbing elbows with generational wealth at that age also inoculated me to its charms; I could see its value, the things it could translate into (for good or bad), but it wasn't this magical ring with infinite power.

On the academic front, I was an average student because I could get by without studying, but I was rarely intellectually engaged. I played sports: I was on the baseball team my sophomore and junior years, Cubans being long-standing baseball fans, where I played first base, third base, and catcher, in that order. Later on, I took up martial arts, particularly muay Thai and Brazilian jujitsu, which I liked because it was both competitive and empowering, but also meditative, with a spiritual aspect. However counterintuitive it may seem, MMA (mixed martial arts) is controlled chaos, and every fighter I ever met was peaceful and always looking for ways to avoid conflict. I saw it as a means to self-improvement.

But for all of that, I was shy, intensely focused, and a bit of a loner. While I had a lot of strong women in my life—my mother, sister, godmother, and aunt—I didn't do much socializing in high school. I didn't have girlfriends, and although I had a few close friends, I would often cancel plans or make up excuses why I couldn't hang out with them, and pretty soon the problem became the solution. I can count on one hand how many parties I went to during my four years of high school. For many people, high school is the time when they start to define themselves and their personalities, blossoming into what they will become in life. Me, I folded in on myself. I found respite in video games, which in time blotted out every other aspect of my high school existence.

I did manage to lose my virginity at a house party when I was sixteen, with the help of alcohol and a girl who was thankfully more experienced than I was. But more and more, I retreated into a private world of video games: online chess, and RTS (real-time strategy) games like *Stronghold* and *Age of Empires*. Like chess, the latter employ military strategy and tactics; you play against opponents of often equal skill, and you juggle an endless universe of probabilities and arcane history in your head all at once. I would break down every round into three parts, like a chess game—opening, middlegame, and endgame—and began to log an archive of responses to every possible scenario. I'm hypercompetitive to begin with, as well as a bit of a nerd, and suddenly here was something I was really good at. And the more I played, the better I got. Pretty soon it was all I was interested in doing. I was routinely playing four, five, six hours at a stretch. Of course, people come home from work and veg out in front of the TV for that long without lasting consequences. But there was nothing passive about this experience. I'd get jacked up and stay that way; once I was in the zone and firing on all cylinders, it felt like every part of me was engaged. This quickly became a vortex I could dive into and disappear.

Except the deeper into it I got, the more I began to experience a creeping uneasiness, one that slowly morphed into feelings of shame. I could slowly sense my real life slipping away. Now there are esports leagues, Twitch, and an entire industry where top players fill stadiums and teens can make six-figure incomes and achieve international stardom. The gaming industry currently generates more income in the United States than movies and sports combined. But back then, video games were still for losers—they didn't have the cachet they would take on in coming years. It created a parallel world for me, and I became something of a recluse. My grades fell off. I quit the baseball team halfway through my senior year and stopped seeing most of my friends. My family could see there was something wrong; it was the same as if I'd had a drug problem. It was a really bad time in my life.

Eventually, the problem eclipsed anything I was getting out of it, and I had to figure out another path forward. With the help of my family, I was able to see that what started out as a hobby had become unhealthy, and I began to disengage from gaming and started to recover my sense of self, apart from the validation I felt in this artificial arena. Shortly after I graduated high school, I began to slowly reduce the amount of time I spent playing. With the sudden lack of regimented activities to occupy my time, I now craved structure and discipline, not to mention this semblance of community I had found online, and for a brief time I seriously considered joining the military. I thought it would restore order and purpose to my life, and that I would be ideally suited to it, given what I had just been through.

Ultimately, I decided that would be impractical. But out of those cravings, I eventually developed an idea I called Gaming Detox, which would be a platform to connect gamers and their families with mental health professionals—something like BetterHelp or Talkspace (direct online portals to match prospective patients and mental health professionals in real time), which didn't exist back then. I realized it was this strong sense of community, encouraged by the rush of endorphins you get from playing, that causes gamers to withdraw from society like I did. You can see it in college dropout rates and all kinds of statistics, and the more I researched it, the more evidence I found for the need for something like this. An ad hoc community and healthier lifestyle would serve as a safety net for those who went all in like I did.

I forged these thoughts into a business plan, born out of my own experiences. I hired a web developer to help me create the website. And this became the big idea I wanted to pursue, something that was mine, that I could carry into the world and make it a better place.

And so I set about trying to find my place in life. I was six feet tall and cleaned up okay. With some effort, I could project confidence. But underneath all of that, I can see now there was a hesitation, an uncertainty. At eighteen, I was technically an adult, but one who had largely missed out on parties, dating, and the robust experiences of late adolescence. The emotional part of me wasn't fully developed yet, and in many ways I was still very immature. Working a series of retail jobs, immersing myself in groups of people my own age, I felt like I had to play catch-up. I read a raft of books on self-improvement, and I rarely turned down invitations from new friends.

I was launching myself into the real world. Whether or not I was prepared for it was an open question.

CHAPTER 3

THE FONTAINEBLEAU

My first job out of high school was at Hollister, an offshoot of Abercrombie & Fitch, the casual wear clothing retailer. A recruiter approached me at a local park while I was doing pull-ups, and when I started working there I fell in with a group of young, attractive people my own age who worked and played together: nightclubs like the Florida Room at the Delano Hotel and LIV at the Fontainebleau; lots of bars and house parties and drinking games like flip cup and beer pong. I enjoyed the work and the feeling of camaraderie with my colleagues. Before I knew it I had new friends, and with them an active social life. I learned my way around Miami nightlife, and I saw more new faces than I had in my entire life. And I developed a taste for whiskey, tequila, and a Brazilian drink called a caipirinha, which is like a margarita made with a sugarcane liqueur called cachaça. And it no longer mattered that I was shy; now women pursued *me*.

At this point, I wasn't interested in college because I saw more value in working and saving money. That last part turned out to be aspirational, on a salary of a hundred dollars a week, with no sales commission. In addition, we were expected to buy Hollister's clothes so we could appear as in-store billboards and ambassadors of the brand.

Working the floor, and curious how such a high-volume business could pay us so little, I began analyzing the operation to see how the money flowed through it. As respectfully as I could, I made my findings known to the manager, breaking it all down for him in a cost-benefit analysis to argue that we were being grossly underpaid. Let's just say this did not go over well, and soon afterward, I jumped over to Abercrombie & Fitch, where the pay was slightly better.

I also started taking a few classes at Miami Dade College, one or two per semester, to see what I was missing—business, accounting, entrepreneurship, hospitality courses, as well as history and philosophy, which it turns out I really liked. My plan was to get a better job so I could save up money to attend one of the schools up north—Florida State University in Tallahassee, or the University of Florida in Gainesville. I applied at a bunch of hotels—first at the Biltmore in Coral Gables, and then a couple of resorts right on the water. I had a friend who worked at the Fontainebleau—that and the adjacent Eden Roc embodied the height of mid-fifties Art Deco glamour—and I asked him if they were hiring. He said they were always looking for recreation attendants, the small army of guys my age who keep the party running smoothly out by the pool. He told me the job paid eleven dollars an hour—already better than what I was pulling down at Abercrombie & Fitch—but that the real money was in tips, which with all the high rollers, both legit and wannabe, could total as much as five hundred dollars a shift.

So I applied for the job, listing my friend as a reference. I had three or four interviews with different managers, and I was very honest: I needed to make money for tuition, and I was willing to work hard to do it; I had retail experience, and I wouldn't get triggered by rude guests (at least they probably wouldn't take their designer T-shirt off and throw it at me, as happened once at A&F). And I had been around rich people socially, so I knew how they liked to be treated. At six feet tall and in peak physical condition, I felt I could defuse any situation that might come up. Management liked the fact I was ambitious, and that I was taking business courses on the side to better myself. They not only offered me a job, but also offered to accommodate my class schedule.

BUILT IN 1954, THE FONTAINEBLEAU IS MIAMI BEACH AT ITS swankiest. Its Art Deco design fused with Vegas glitz—"Miami Modern," I guess is the correct term—where Jerry Lewis starred as *The Bellboy*, Frank Sinatra welcomed Elvis home from the army on live television, and Tony Montana got a lesson in how to pick up women poolside in *Scarface*. Although it had faced bankruptcy in the early seventies, a two-year, $2 billion renovation in 2008 had restored this onetime architectural treasure to its former glory, all of which would soon be reflected in the clientele.

I worked the pool area—a main pool with cabanas along

the side, a nightclub/lounge, and a couple of smaller pools at either end. I wore the required uniform of shorts, a white cotton T-shirt, and a baseball cap, to try and mitigate the punishing Miami sun. My job was to fold towels and hand them out wherever they were requested or needed; rearrange or reserve chairs, all of which came at a premium; and to find or accomplish whatever a guest might need at any given time. Mainly, the job was to treat them like they wanted to be treated—like they imagined they ought to be treated—a privilege for which they were more than happy to pay a handsome dividend.

In any hospitality business, there's a low season and a high season. Low season, it's slow; no one is motivated, there's no action, which means no tips. It's like a nightclub where it's too early in the evening—nothing is happening yet. People call in sick, sneak out early, bitch about their jobs. High season clocks in around November and carries on through April. December is when all the snowbirds come, and they tip well, and it's also when the celebrities show up. The celebrities draw the high rollers, or else they are the high rollers; either way, that draws women, and before long there is no shortage of beautiful people. The high season makes up for the rest of the year.

The scene is designed to be one big pool party. At noon, the DJ kicks in and music starts blasting, and everything gets a little looser. Arcadia, a private club adjacent to the main pool area with its own smaller pool and cabana, starts in with a soundtrack and pumped-up vibe, and that continues all the way into the evening, where nightclub impresario David Grutman runs LIV, a dance club on the premises, which brings in some of the most famous DJs in the world. It also attracts major players: Jay-Z spent over $250,000 on bottle service and tipped the waitstaff

$50,000 in addition to the guaranteed 18 percent tip, which is included in all tabs.

In this environment, if you're in one of the cabanas, and you are entertaining friends who start showing up by early afternoon, you will require a constant stream of bottles from the bar and food from the kitchen. As a result, it's not that difficult to drop a profound amount of money. A $10,000 tab was not uncommon. Factor in the social lubricants of alcohol and a party atmosphere and people could become very generous with their tips.

Servers make the most money. Sometimes, you'd have guests spend $20,000 at a cabana over the course of a week. There's limited space, so every single chair is valuable, too. As per custom, and the implicit backing of the house, a hundred dollar tip would secure you a chair for the day, which we reserved with a folded towel and personal items stacked on top. Regulars know the rules, so you reserve them their chairs first thing in the morning for the duration of their stay. This would automatically build relationships between guests and staff, and I'm fortunate enough to have a good memory for faces and names. It's like being a good bartender; familiarity ingratiates you with the clientele, which leads to better tips.

When you clock in, management gives you the lay of the land: "This company reserved this entire area; make sure they have everything they need." "Grey Goose is hosting a promotion for a new product line. See to it that people know about it." They tell you what section you'll be in, what drinks they're pushing, and especially where the VIPs are located. Just like in Las Vegas, these are returning customers who are heavy hitters and likely to drop a lot of money. The whales.

I've seen Floyd Mayweather tip a thousand dollars. People like that—boxing champions, NBA basketball stars, NFL football players, soccer prodigies, tennis stars—burn through cash because they want to be treated like kings or queens. And why shouldn't they? There's nothing arbitrary about why they're in this position; they're not accidental celebrities, where fame fell out of the sky one day and landed on top of them, or heirs to somebody else's random fortune. What's a couple hundred dollars to them? They are there to be seen. Staff can carry on a conversation with them, maybe become friendly and connect with them on a human level. But I always made sure to lead with respect and see that they got whatever they needed. Then I'm "their guy." It all goes to back to Sinatra and the Rat Pack, who made this place one of their main ports of call. Bottle service, bloody steaks, cigar rooms, the trappings of wealth—everybody's chasing the same feeling. I saw a Jersey mob type at the bar once handing out Rolexes to his whole crew; he had twenty of them in boxes. Sinatra could be a world-class jerk, but he famously slipped a fifty dollar bill to everyone he met.

And then there are the women. Brazilian women, Colombian women, Argentinian women; beautiful women from all corners of the globe, but especially Central and South America. They dressed in thong bikinis and high heels and sunglasses, which they know how to artfully peer over the tops of. It's breathtaking; it can literally stop you in your tracks.

There are multiple shifts, so if I worked the early shift, I had to show up at 4:00 a.m., long before first light, where it's not uncommon to see couples having sex in the pool. Flirting between guests and hotel staff was pretty common, especially with men and women with the means and the interest in having some fun. There were times when I'd have a bachelorette party going while there was a group of guys in one of the cabanas looking to meet women, with money to burn, but without the confidence or skill set to initiate contact on their own. Acting as their roving ambassador on my official rounds, it was easy to approach the group of single women and ask, "You guys want some free drinks?"

Their answer would inevitably be "Yeah!"

"Well then, follow me." I'd lead them to the men's cabana, make the introductions, the liquor would flow, and the guys would tip me, heavily and discreetly. Now the women were happy, the guys were happy, and I was everybody's new best friend.

Of course, the work itself was brutal. Imagine going to the beach for a couple of hours, and how you feel afterward. Now multiply that by four for an eight-hour shift. I was constantly on the move, running, hustling, carrying chairs and umbrellas on my back. By the end of a shift, my feet would routinely be bloody and covered in blisters. I'd get home every night exhausted and depleted.

But I met the most interesting people. As a twenty-year-old looking to understand how business works and how to make money, I was intrigued by those who had achieved a measure of success; they spoke its language and could tell its stories. If they're staying in a suite that costs a couple thousand dollars a night, and spending hundreds more on food and drink, then anything they choose to impart to you is received as wisdom. To get through the front door alone, they had to know something you didn't: how to get from there to here.

I routinely recognized the CEOs, high-level executives, entrepreneurs, and self-made millionaires I had read about in the business press. As I interacted with them, I would observe how they thought, how they approached problem-solving. If I was interested, and if they recognized some of those same qualities in me, maybe they'd sit and talk with me during my downtime. Professors can teach you economic theory, but most have no practical experience with business success, the way, say, an architect or engineer can leaven their technical knowledge with time in the trenches. Otherwise, they wouldn't be professors.

Management recognized I was passing through, ideally on my way somewhere more fulfilling. Or maybe I would stay and climb the corporate ladder there. Hundreds of million dollars moved through the hotel on an annual basis, and since they knew I was taking business classes at night, managers would go out of their way to share details of the inner workings when I asked. Self-confidence probably helped, as I was becoming more and more assured, breaking out of my shell.

Whatever my future held, I felt like I finally had a vantage point to see how it might unfold, and the vista held promise. Until one day in March 2012, when everything changed.

CHAPTER 4

HELLO, MY NAME IS GIANCARLO

At the tail end of the high season, on March 13, 2012, I was close to ending my shift at around 4:00 p.m., when I fell into a conversation with one of the guests. She lived in Dallas, was around my age (I was about to turn twenty-one), and I could tell she liked it when I flirted with her. She explained how she and her girlfriend were there on vacation, and she gave me her phone number. I had never hooked up with one of the guests before, and never would again after that day. I flew out to visit her later on, and spent a week hanging out and meeting her friends, but the distance ultimately proved too daunting.

In the midst of doing my job, while circling back around to say a few more words to the girl from Dallas, I noticed a woman staring at me. She was camped out in my section—maybe in her mid-forties, attractive, fit, and very charismatic—stretched out on one of the poolside daybeds in a bikini. Daybeds are way more comfortable than the lounge chairs, and the going rate was $150 a day, so anyone with a daybed already had my attention.

Her dark brown eyes locked on to me, and I felt her watching me wherever I went. She had a deep, penetrating stare, and when she caught my eye she didn't look away. It was a little disconcerting. The next time I was within earshot, she said, "Oh, these girls don't know what they're doing. You need someone older."

She was being flirty, saying it as a joke, so I flirted back—standard procedure on my part. She asked my name, and when I shook her hand, she complimented me on my handshake. We talked for a few minutes—"Do you go to school?"; "What kind of stuff are you interested in?"—and then I told her I had to get back to work. Every time I cycled through, there was a little more banter and a little more flirtation. She said her name was Becki. She had a very inviting personality, and right off the bat she seemed like a lot of fun. I thought she might have been competing with the girl from Dallas, but as far as I could tell the other girl wasn't paying attention to us.

It all seemed innocent enough, but then near the end of my shift, she asked me to sit down next to her on the daybed, where nobody could hear us, and in a conspiratorial tone asked me, "Hey, do you want to come back to my room?"

Not what I was expecting.

When I didn't say no right away, she added, "There's just one thing . . . My husband wants to watch."

There was a lot to unpack in that sentence: a sexy rendezvous is about to happen, but wait, she's married, but no, her husband's okay with it and in fact he's coming along to have a look. That was too many hairpin turns, and the resulting whiplash made me a little queasy.

She knew it was shocking, and there was a slight catch in her voice when she said it. I must have recoiled ever so slightly, because she was quick to add, "Oh don't worry, he'll hide in the corner and watch us. That's his thing. You won't even know he's there."

By way of explanation, she said that she and her husband had visited Miami Velvet, a local swingers club in Doral. A lot of swingers stayed at the Fontainebleau, so Miami Velvet was well known to all of us who worked there. She confessed they had been curious about those sorts of places, having had no experience with them, but it was all gross, nothing sensual or erotic about it, people having faceless mechanical sex everywhere you looked, so they left. All I really knew about Miami Velvet was that it served as a punch line for the locals. I had never known anyone who had actually been there, and I had the sense that it was for an older age group. But now the conversation was charged with sex, and I wanted her to stay on topic.

I was conflicted. On the one hand, she was in her bikini, touching her neck, fussing with her hair, paying me compliments, sipping on her drink while she stared into my eyes. I found it all very intriguing. But it was also weird and unlike anything I had ever done before. I asked her if we could meet up alone first, but she said that would go against their agreement. I told her I needed some time to think about it and asked her to call me after my shift, which ended in another hour. She typed my number into her phone. She didn't give me hers.

I had seen her surreptitiously taking pictures of me, in between chatting me up, and I surmised that she must have been texting her husband the whole time. Later, after she sent me a batch of the photos, I realized that at least one of them was taken from outside my section, which means she would have had to move *into* my section, which I suppose makes it a surveillance photo.

Soon after, her husband came down and joined us, and she introduced him as Jerry. He wore Speedo briefs, with his belly hanging over his waistband. It was a little awkward, and he largely avoided eye contact, but he shook my hand and said, "Nice to meet you, Gian," with his thick southern accent. He pronounced Gian like "John," and this became his nickname for me for as long as I knew him.

Some of my coworkers and at least one manager could see what was going on, and they encouraged me to go for it. We all agreed it was strange but also hilarious. When Jerry left, he told me he'd see me later.

In the parking lot my cell buzzed and the number came up as blocked. It was Becki. She had mentioned that they were staying in a suite in the Trésor Tower, which is between $1,000 and $1,500 a night, so while I didn't know who they were, they obviously had money. Still, they suggested we meet at a Days Inn around the corner from the Fontainebleau so we could avoid any issues with hotel management if anybody recognized me. With traffic, it took me an hour to get home to my parents' house, shower, and change into jeans and a black T-shirt, and then a half hour to get back. I called my sister on my way home and told her what was happening, including what hotel we would be at, in case Becki and Jerry turned out to be serial killers. She thought the whole thing was hysterical. She was in her late twenties at this point, and a confidant and best friend, so she knew all about my dating life. She asked me, "Do you think this is a good idea?" laughing as she said it. I told her, "Probably not." But then, you're only twenty once.

I arrived at the Days Inn around 8:30 or 9:00 p.m. Becki was sitting on a couch in the lobby. I was nervous, and I guess she was too, because she poured whiskey from a fifth of Jack Daniel's into a plastic cup. She wore nightclub attire: a tight dress that finished at mid-thigh, not see-through but suggestive, and black heels. We passed the cup back and forth between us to calm our nerves.

At one point, she said, "I can't believe we're going to do this. This is crazy." At the time I had the impression they had never done this before, but a decade later I think that's highly unlikely. For starters, if this was Jerry's "thing," how exactly did they come by this knowledge? Regardless, we made small talk as she lightly stroked my arms and inner thigh. I rested my hand on her leg, and soon we were comfortable enough with each other that she told me, "All right, let's go upstairs." On the elevator up she backed up against me, and I folded my arms around her.

I followed her into a clean, generic room with two queen-size beds. Jerry lay on the one closest to the door, dressed, but with his jeans unbuttoned and fanned open so you could see his underwear; shoes off, with his shirtsleeves rolled up to the elbows. It was awkward at first, but he was already drunk, and he greeted me with "Hey, Gian," and then let out a giggle. That was a little disconcerting, but it also served to break the ice, since it added to the absurdity. He had a drink, which he kept sipping while we talked.

I told him, "If you get jealous at any point, just let me know and I'll get the hell out of here. I will not hesitate." I was still worried that he might attack me and stave in the back of my head.

But he told me, "Don't worry about it. You guys do what you want to do."

I kissed Becki, and she was practically vibrating. I picked her up and carried her over to the second bed. She was surprisingly light. She wasn't wearing any panties, which is the kind of thing that makes an impression on you at twenty, and she half whispered, "Our rule is anything but intercourse," meaning no penetration. I nodded that was fine. I went down on her, and when she finished, she told me, "My turn. Lay back."

At some point, Jerry got up and walked to the side of the bed to get a better angle. I had a moment of near panic, thinking, *What is he doing?* and I told him to back off—not in a hostile way, just establishing some boundaries. He apologized and quickly walked back toward the entrance and stood right outside the bathroom. After that I was able to put blinders on and block him out. Becki rarely lost eye contact with me, but for all her forwardness, she seemed submissive in the moment, eager to please.

Afterward, they were elated that we'd managed to pull it off. She was buzzing, electric, and Jerry continued to giggle with excitement. I was happy, but this was enough pathfinding for one day. I told them, "All right, guys—I'm outta here." Becki kissed me on the lips and then walked me down to the lobby. As I drove home, I was pretty sure I'd never hear from them again.

The next day, my cell phone rang as I was walking across campus. I picked up to hear Becki's voice.

"Hey, what's up?" she said. "You want to see me again before I leave?"

I paused, then thought, *Why not?* When I told her yes, she invited me to their suite in the Trésor Tower. It was my day off from work, and I'd just gotten out of class, so what the hell. I told her I could be there in an hour.

I went in through the street entrance in civilian clothes so I wouldn't run in to any of my coworkers. Becki was waiting for me in the lobby again and took me up to the room. This time, as soon as the door closed, she asked me about my day, and as I started to answer her, she slipped my jeans down and performed oral sex on me. Jerry lurked in the corner, mostly invisible in the shadows. I'm pretty sure he masturbated, but if he didn't then, he certainly did later on in the relationship. After I finished, they both started peppering me with questions: How old was I? Where did I go to school? Did I have a girlfriend? I said, "I'm not twenty-one yet." They both got very quiet, until I added, "But I am twenty, and yeah, I'm enrolled in college at Miami Dade." They could tell I was messing with them, and that eased the lingering awkwardness, since it was the middle of the day and we hadn't started with drinks to get us in the mood. Becki laughed and said, "I was hoping you weren't like seventeen or something."

We talked about my college experience, still limited at that point, with Jerry taking a particular interest. He was adamant on the value of a college degree, and how it would help me in the long run. I asked them what they did, and Jerry said he was an attorney and ran his own business. When I asked him what business, he said "a school," and then at my prodding, "a university." He tried to sound nonchalant when he said it, but it didn't seem like he wanted to get into it, so I let it drop. They said they helped a lot of young people, and encouraged me to call them if I ever needed any guidance. The three of us exchanged numbers, and they told me "We'll be in touch." This time, I found my own way back downstairs.

Despite the wild circumstances, I felt a legitimate chemistry between the three of us. I found myself attracted to Becki, and as weird as it was, Jerry seemed like a decent guy. We all got along well, and I felt comfortable around both of them.

That night, Jerry sent me a text from their room in the Trésor Tower. It read, "Hey Gian! Hope all is well with you. Becki asked me to send you these pictures. Have a good night. Jerry." One was of Jerry and me, and the other was of Becki and me. We all looked very happy.

The next day, Jerry and Becki departed for the airport and flew back to Lynchburg, Virginia, on a private jet with their children and two other couples, who had been with them the whole time.

I've since wondered if I dove headfirst into this precisely because of what I'd missed out on in high school. Your teenage years are when most people engage with the world, but somehow I did the opposite. More specifically, I can't help but wonder if this is what the Falwells detected in me—that tentativeness I felt toward life. Maybe to the trained eye, I seemed like I was searching for guidance, mentorship, molding. I didn't know it then, but these people were the stewards of a large university; they were constantly around young people. Perhaps they spotted my insecurity and knew how to exploit my vulnerabilities.

The night I met them, Becki started texting, which continued for the duration of the relationship. She also gave me five stars in her Tripadvisor review:

> Giancarlo did an amazing job setting up our bed and making sure our towels were fresh and dry. He was also very knowledgeable about hotel amenities and eager to share information with us. It was obvious that he is a very conscientious and competent young man . . . There was always someone nearby to pick up trash or help with anything that was needed. This truly was one of the highlights of our trip. Thanks, Becki.

CHAPTER 5

AROUND THE WORLD

The Falwells invited me to come and spend the weekend with them at the Cheeca Lodge & Spa in Islamorada on April 5, roughly three weeks after we first met. In between, I turned twenty-one on March 28. (Becki had recently turned forty-seven and Jerry was coming up on his fiftieth birthday.) Becki told me, "We want to see you again; we can't stop thinking about you." This time, their kids—sons Trey and Wesley, a year apart and just older and younger than me, respectively, and daughter Caroline, who was eleven—would stay separately at the Fontainebleau.

Islamorada was near the southern end of the Florida Keys, the long tail of connected islands off the South Florida coast, and a couple hours' drive from where I lived, so it was easy for me to meet them there. I took the whole weekend off and headed down.

In addition to all the texting with Becki—flirting mostly, with a fair amount of sexual tension, or else updates on their daily activities, sometimes four or five times a day—we also spoke by phone every single day, usually for an hour or so. Never phone sex and no sexting. Mainly getting to know one another, like you would during a proper courtship. I would take long walks so my parents wouldn't overhear us. They figured out something was going on anyway, since the phone bill had all these long-distance calls from the same Virginia number. Sometimes Jerry would get on and say a few words, ask me how school was going or how my day had been. I also had the feeling that even when he didn't speak up, he was listening in on the line.

We stayed at the Oceanside Bungalow, with back steps that led directly down onto the beach. The accommodations were on a par with the Fontainebleau, if a little more sedate. With presidents Harry Truman and George Bush Sr. among its many famous guests, it was a place you'd go for a family vacation or a romantic getaway, so no groups of single girls or guys pounding down Patrón shots at the cabana bar. That first night, we had dinner at an Italian restaurant on the grounds, and things were comfortable between the three of us. There was none of that nervous, jagged energy from before.

After dinner, we retired to the pool area, where Becki started kissing and caressing me in the hot tub. I worried that someone would see us, and told her so, but she didn't seem concerned about it. They genuinely didn't think anyone would care. She kissed my chest and stroked my inner thigh and told me to stop worrying. They both drank a lot, with Jerry enjoying his Coke and Bacardi Oakheart (a spiced rum), and Becki her vodka and Baileys Irish Cream (essentially a white Russian). Sometimes it was Baileys and coffee if it was early or late enough. I stuck to tequila on the rocks. After we were suitably marinated, we went back to the bungalow.

This was the first time we went all the way, with Jerry taking up his perch in the corner. There was still the residual feeling of *Is this really happening?* But as the weekend wore on, it started to feel more like normal sex, or like a regular affair, even with a third party in the room. Since the room only had a single king-size bed, Jerry slept on an air mattress on the floor, leaving Becki and me the bed.

We spent the weekend swimming, paddleboarding, kayaking, hiking, and biking, while in between, Becki and I would slip away and hook up multiple times a day. Jerry made his presence less obtrusive, or else he left us alone altogether. He would retreat to the pool or read in the lobby while she and I had sex. Observers have tried to call it a ménage à trois, but that is not accurate. Whatever the bargain was between them, it didn't have much to do with me. They clearly both got something out of it, but Becki was almost always the instigator. She picked the time and the place, and to the extent that this was a habit with them, she picked the guy. Jerry was just along for the ride. She told me once she'd never really had another boyfriend besides Jerry, so maybe she was reliving the youth she wished she'd had. Jerry would often tell me she needed a boyfriend, or a confidant or whatever.

Or maybe Jerry was only trying to provide for her needs and her robust fantasy life, even if it took them into some strange territory. She had an insatiable sexual appetite and a crazy libido.

Jerry would joke publicly that he couldn't keep up with Becki, that she was too much. I saw that firsthand. But at least with me, she was always generous, eager to please, and she took pleasure in seeing that I was satisfied. Lots of back rubs, massages, a willingness to try new things. She made you feel like a million bucks. And she would mix things up; she liked it when I controlled things, she liked to be dominated. I'm reminded of what she said the first time we met: those young girls don't know how to treat a man. What I was responding to was her experience.

Cheeca was also where Becki first told me she loved me. It was at the Italian restaurant at the lodge. Jerry was there. She started out by saying, "I don't want to freak you out," and then Jerry smiled when she said it. It was a little shocking to hear. I didn't come from a family where people said that casually; we barely hugged, and now here was this person I'd only recently met telling me things I'd never heard or said. I had never told a girlfriend I loved her because, up to that point, I'd never had a girlfriend. I thought, *Is this how adults do this?* And then she wanted me to say it back to her. I told them I didn't feel comfortable saying it, but she insisted. She told me, "Just say it—it'll feel good." I reluctantly mumbled, "I love you," and Becki said, "You see? It's not that hard. It'll get easier the more we say it." It was awkward, and Jerry smiled and said, "Becki has a big heart. She's like a golden retriever that needs constant love and attention."

I learned later on this is called "love bombing," and it's a tactic narcissists use early in a relationship: excessive flattery, hyperattentiveness, over-the-top affection. All of it is designed to overwhelm the recipient, paralyze their natural defenses, and isolate them from the comforting elements of their life. I can see now it was all conditioning: the daily texts and phone calls leading up to this moment were trying to make an artificial situation—strangers suddenly thrown into a false intimacy— seem more normal by forcing it into a familiar pattern. All the while, they acted like this was all new to them, and we were all trying to figure it out together. They were teaching me the particulars of this new intimacy they were exploring as we went along. And at least part of me was anxious to learn.

But who's to say she didn't believe it—at least in the moment? Even though it's highly unlikely this was their first rodeo, after everything that's happened and everything I know about her, I still believe she allowed herself to fall in love a little bit. Or if not love exactly, then at least obsession. I might not have had the experience yet to make that call, but I lived through it, and I've thought about it a lot since, and that's how it seemed to me.

Aside from all of that, I still maintain Jerry, Becki, and I had a natural rapport. They can say whatever they want about me today, but I always felt like the three of us were very compatible as friends. On that trip I also saw Jerry as his own person, separate from Becki. He opened up more, and I learned that he was the president of Liberty University, essentially the largest Christian university in the world. He talked to me about business and the multimillion-dollar real estate deals he routinely managed. The conversations were like those I had with the businessmen poolside at the Fontainebleau, but in far more detail—all of which I soaked up like a sponge. He'd talk about the board, managing competing power interests and outsize personalities, the donors and various benefactors.

For someone like me who was interested in the ins and outs of business, and who scraped together money to buy shares in

Facebook and Tesla and routinely read their annual reports, these conversations were fascinating and extremely informative. I was familiar with many of the people and concepts he brought up, and I have a good memory, so I could absorb much of what he was telling me, allowing him to cover a lot of ground in a single sitting. It was a heady feeling that he would trust me with his insider perspective.

Jerry and Becki were the first people outside of my family I told about being addicted to video games in high school, and about my Gaming Detox idea. With his proximity to lots of young people through Liberty University, I wanted Jerry's input. It was therapeutic for me as much as anything. Gaming, not to mention being addicted to it, was a dark secret back then—certainly within my peer group. All that time I spent holed up in my room, rejecting real life for a cheesy simulacrum. It was embarrassing to talk about. But Jerry didn't judge. He said my idea sounded like a viable business opportunity, and that I should partner with Liberty on it, which was unbelievably validating.

The more we talked, that weekend and then later on, Jerry would say things like "You remind me of me when I was younger" or "I see a lot of myself in you." He told me he wanted to "pay it forward": When he was in law school at the University of Virginia in the mid-eighties, he interned for an attorney who presented him with a thirty-day option on twenty-two acres of land near a local mall for $220,000. A local businessman agreed to partner with Jerry, and they bought the land and built town houses on it, all of which sold quickly. Jerry brought in his cousin, used their initial success as collateral for a loan from a local bank, used that loan to buy out his original partner, bought more parcels of land, and built more town houses. The money printed itself, and by the time they were through, he had made $700,000 and earned himself a reputation as a successful deal-maker. None of which would have happened without someone with resources taking a chance on him. Now he said he wanted to do the same with me.

Over time, I learned a lot from our talks. Whatever else you want to say about him, Jerry is brilliant in business. He's extremely smart and has sound commercial judgment, with an eye for real estate development. Liberty University may be a personal piggy bank for his family, but he's widely credited with taking the school from near bankruptcy to where it stands now, with an estimated $2 billion endowment. He accomplished this mainly by adding the online component in 2009, sometimes referred to as "distance learning," which increased the university's enrollment sevenfold and made it solvent. That's quite an accomplishment. At times he would let me listen in on conference calls with developers. Simply hearing how he ran the meetings and coped with the various roadblocks he encountered, or kept competing interests at bay while moving complicated deals forward, was all very educational.

Eventually, once I got a handle on the concepts and the details of individual deals, I could act as a sounding board for him. Not an adviser, since I knew a fraction of what he knew. But on occasion I could offer a new perspective or confirm what he already suspected. At times, we'd take long hikes, and he would spin out the evolution of various projects he was working on. With me, he could discuss things in almost granular detail and not run the risk of boring me. I don't know if that was true of anyone else. Maybe his sons, Trey and Wesley, both of whom eventually fell into the family business, but I don't know that they had it in their blood like I did. I had taken accounting courses in high school, which is the foundation of most business, and I enjoyed analyzing operations and how things worked. He liked that. I would get it on the back channel from Becki: "You know, Jerry is really impressed with you. He likes the fact that you know about business and actually care."

Jerry was not like a lot of the people I've met who have money. He always picked up the check—not ostentatiously, or to ingratiate himself for some favor later on, but so everyone else wouldn't have to worry about it. He didn't seem to care about money all that much. I'm sure they both appreciated the good life. Above a certain level, money is a game, and a way of keeping score (or else settling scores). But for a lot of people, money is also exclusive; it makes your life into a giant party you can throw for no better reason than to keep everybody else out. That sort of snobbery wasn't really something he indulged in. If anything, they were inclusive—if they threw a party, everyone was welcome.

By this point, I knew they were heads of a large religious university and that Jerry's father had been a famous evangelical preacher. But there was no discussion of church that weekend, or religion, or theological concepts. To tell you the truth, I'm not even sure they were all that religious. They certainly didn't subscribe to the same puritanical constraints the university placed on its student body, a code of behavior known as the Liberty Way. I'm convinced that's why Jerry didn't follow in his father's footsteps as a man of the cloth like his brother, Jonathan, did. He was happy serving behind the scenes as a lawyer and developer, only taking a leadership position at Liberty upon his father's demise in 2007.

He and Becki both believed in God, and they would talk about it if you asked them, but they didn't go to church unless there was a visiting dignitary or some other circumstance that made their presence essential. They said they had a personal relationship with God, and they didn't need the trappings or the ritual. Jerry told me during one of his business deals, "If anyone brings God into business, don't trust them." At one point, they feared I might be an atheist, and Becki encouraged me to try and believe. But that was the extent of their evangelical impulse. Whenever I was in Lynchburg, where your religious identity is always hanging in the air above you, they would say, "Just tell them you're Catholic." The only time I ever heard Becki intone the Lord's name was when she told me, "God put us together for a reason."

Jerry was a chess player, and we played often. We were fairly evenly matched, although I more often resorted to reckless gambits. Our games often ended in a draw. This contributed to Jerry's apparent growing respect for me and our mutual bonding. He enjoyed the competition and the strategy of the game. I appreciated the mentorship of someone who had prevailed in life. And Jerry was like my dad (or at least how I imagined other dads to be), spurring me on to greater things.

The weekend went great. We were beginning to bond, and they were interesting people to get to know. They wanted to do it again as soon as possible, and I agreed. I bought plane tickets, and on April 25, I flew to New York and met them at the Gansevoort Hotel at 420 Park Avenue South (now the Royalton Park Avenue), just off Times Square. This was ostensibly to discuss my idea for Gaming Detox, and how I could partner with them on it. In a remarkably short period of time, they had transformed from swingers into potential investors. I shared the exciting news with my coworkers at the Fontainebleau, my family, my friends—anyone who would listen.

That first night, we had dinner at the STK Steakhouse in Midtown. Once again, this being Manhattan, I was concerned the paparazzi might get a shot of us going in and we'd all end up in the tabloids. But they were both confident they'd only be spotted in their own world: in Lynchburg or around the university. It seemed reckless to me, but I wasn't in a position to lecture them about it. Jerry said they would be meeting up later with John Regan of Permanens Capital and Joe Steinberg, both from the investment committee at Liberty, which managed the university's endowment. Jerry suggested we schedule meetings with both to discuss my idea, although that ultimately didn't happen.

Just like our last trip, Becki and I had sex multiple times a day with Jerry looking on, while in between the three of us explored the neighborhood, talked business in the rooftop bar, with its corner view of the Empire State Building, and swam in the rooftop pool with a giant image of Marilyn Monroe wrapped in a towel emblazoned on the tiled bottom. Since the Cheeca trip at the beginning of the month, we'd had several phone calls about how Liberty might provide the infrastructure I needed to help my business plan come together. They put me in touch with Dr. Tim Clinton, a psychologist at the university, who gave me a book called *The Digital Invasion*. (I'm holding it in a photo taken in front of Liberty's private jet that made the papers soon after my story went public.) Liberty had experienced a falloff in male enrollment, which a recent study had attributed to the proliferation of video games, and he saw my proposal as a potential bulwark against any further slide in their numbers. But on the second day of our discussions, Jerry sized Gaming Detox up as follows: "I think it's a really great idea, but it's going to take you a little while to make money. You need to start making money now."

As an alternative, he suggested I search for a property in South Beach that we could partner on. He said he wanted to diversify their portfolio, and with my knowledge of the area, if I kept an eye out for potential bargains, he was confident I could find the right opportunity. And he could guarantee me an equity stake worth at least 25 percent of any investment in the $5 million range. He also said he would like his son Trey—Jerry Falwell III—to be involved in the deal. I was aware that whatever deal he suggested would align with some internal agenda I might not be privy to, and probably wouldn't realize until long after the fact. It would have to check certain boxes, and no doubt serve multiple purposes. But I didn't necessarily see that as a bad thing. Maybe it would help explain my presence around his family; Trey and I were roughly the same age—maybe we'd hit it off and then I'd become Trey's friend. But it didn't have to be nefarious; it only had to fit into his overall strategy. If I was loyal, honest, and appreciated the opportunity—and if I was someone he could count on in the future—then that was what I brought to the table. Those were my assets. I wasn't simply Becki's playmate who he had to keep entertained during her downtime. It was more like we were all becoming friends and now we were going to be colleagues.

I'm not convinced Jerry ever really understood the business model for Gaming Detox. But if your future business partners are trying to let you down easy, the prospect of a quarter share in what would eventually become a $7 million commercial property in the heart of a South Beach boomtown helps to soften the blow. They started using phrases like, "After you make your first million . . . ," which renders the rest of that sentence moot.

Except I'm pretty sure a good businessman always keeps an escape hatch in plain sight. Now I was all in. And soon enough, it would be impossible to go back to my old life.

CHAPTER 6

CRAZY EX-GIRLFRIEND

After Gansevoort, Becki and I got together as often as logistics would allow. They would fly down to Miami and stay at the Loews Hotel in South Beach, and later on, I would visit them in Lynchburg, as well as tag along on their family vacations. Eventually, it got to the point where Becki and I didn't want Jerry in the room with us at all when we did it. We finally told him, "This is too awkward. Can it just be us?" And Becki didn't want him there any more than I did, because the sex was so much better. It's the difference between enjoying yourself and performing for an audience. Or rather, trying not to perform for an audience. Either way, you're going to be more inhibited and self-conscious. This way we could be free to do whatever we wanted. When we finally told him, he seemed like he had been expecting it, and he got up and silently left the room.

Becki and I had maybe fifty separate rendezvous over the next eight years, with some notable time-outs, and I'd say two-thirds of those were Becki and me by ourselves. Of course, there were times when Jerry couldn't help himself and he begged us to let him watch from the corner. I cringe thinking about this, but sometimes he would get so turned on that he would have sex with Becki as soon as I had finished. They both confessed separately that it was a sexless marriage, and they credited me with reinvigorating the intimacy between them. Or that's what they said anyway. Eventually, sex with Becki slowly became normalized, since we were either spending time together or else in constant contact. It was like we were dating, or I had a steady girlfriend.

That all changed when I got my first actual girlfriend.

In May 2012, I met a woman my own age, whom I'll call "Olivia." (I won't name any of my ex-girlfriends here: They didn't sign up for a life of media scrutiny, and they certainly don't need to be thrust back into the public eye. I wouldn't wish that on my worst enemy, and these are people who, by and large, I remember fondly.) She was a couple of years younger than me, and of Cuban descent. A friend of a friend and a med student, she also attended Miami Dade College, where she was on a neuroscience track, and we ended up dating for a little over a year. At first it was casual; we would go out with a group of friends—bowling or to see a movie. In the context of a larger group there was less pressure, and by July we decided to make it official.

During one of our conference calls, I told Jerry and Becki that I had a girlfriend now and I couldn't sleep with Becki anymore. It felt like cheating to me. "So, you're replacing me with someone younger, huh?" Becki said. Then she added, "Jerry, tell him something."

Jerry jumped in, saying, "Gian, I don't blame you." And then to placate Becki: "Of course he's going to date girls in college."

"I know, but it's still hard on me. I don't know what I'm going to do without you, Gian."

I couldn't believe this conversation. I tried to mollify her. "I can still call and text you," I told her. "Everything will stay the same, except for no sex."

Then she began to cry. "You have no idea how much I love you. . . . I need you! Please don't leave me."

"I won't leave you," I said. "I promise."

Jerry said he was going to bed and would leave us to hash it out. I told Becki she should get some sleep, too.

"I just wanted to say that I love you so much. You have no idea how much. Of course you're going to date girls your own age. I'll just have to accept that."

I was relieved. "I'm glad you understand."

We said our good nights, and I felt better about things. Olivia and I were a couple now. Despite their constant encouragements, I held firm about the sex. Becki continued to text me multiple times a day. Mostly it was innocent flirtation:

"Right now I am just missing you like crazy." Or "You're perfect."

Or in case I didn't get the message, this one from July 17:

"Seeing you in person and looking at you in the eyes makes me want to rip your clothes off and get the sh** f***** out of me."

In addition, a new, more insidious tone crept into our conversations. At one point, she left a message for me to call her back, telling me it was urgent, which I did immediately, but she didn't pick up. Then a half hour later, she texted me the following:

"Sorry I missed your calls. I was in the shower . . . all alone! Sorry if I alarmed you. I was watching some video clips on my phone. Wow!! There are two people that are very passionate at lovemaking! . . . Have you had this effect on all your lady friends?"

In case her meaning wasn't clear, the next morning she texted:

"Thinking about you, seeing your picture or watching those amazing videos gets me hot."

So they had videos of me. Or at least she said they did. Taken surreptitiously, and without my knowledge. With Jerry propped in the corner of the room, somewhere in the shadows, and me trying my best to pretend he wasn't there, it would have been easy for him to film with his phone at Cheeca or the Gansevoort without being discovered. And if they recorded us having sex, they might do anything with the footage: send the clip to my parents or my sister. My brand-new girlfriend. My college dean or potential employers. They could obscure Becki's face and then dump the video on the internet or porn sites. It was something they could hold over my head indefinitely, to force me to meet whatever demands they had at any given moment. I felt frightened, embarrassed, vulnerable, and alone, like I had no one I could turn to—not even my sister. I was ashamed that I had let this happen to me. And just in case I thought she was bluffing, Becki sent me a still of us kissing on a hotel bed either at Cheeca or the Gansevoort.

After a while, once I'd calmed down, I decided I was being

silly. They had more to lose from this than I did. Erring on the side of caution, I took all of Becki's texts, at the least the ones I still had or could find, and emailed them to myself so that I would have a record. If they had illicit videos of me, then I had their Mafia-style threats to offer up in my defense. Although we never spoke of it, it locked us into a covenant of mutually assured destruction.

And to be fair: I was having an illicit affair with an older woman with the consent and support of her husband, which seemed ill advised in every possible way. They were twice my age, rich, and powerful public figures, and stalwart paragons of Christian probity. That was half the fun of it—for me *and* them—that it was wrong on so many levels. Should I have been surprised they were recording us? Sex tapes may well have been par for the course. You buy the ticket, you take the ride.

Except what if I were somebody's twenty-one-year-old daughter? What if an older man seduced me, became momentarily obsessed with me, and I knew better but went ahead with it anyway on a whim. It was just some life adventure that presented itself, the kind that I might not have an opportunity for later on, and I was hungry for life. What did it matter? Only to find out that he secretly recorded me having sex, and used it to make demands on me, probably for more sex, then for me to become some kind of sex slave or his emotional support animal or God knows what? Maybe he just wanted to show the tape to all his friends, brag about his conquests or sexual prowess. Maybe his wife was even cool with it, it worked for the both of them, and she started pressuring me to keep it going. And what if at the end of the day, I became some sort of national punch line— further degraded for submitting to this abuse? It's not about gender; it's about the abuse of power. I felt like Monica Lewinsky. And if it were my daughter—*or* son—I'm not sure what I would do. Probably something I would regret.

Despite the fact that we'd agreed to break off intimate relations, Becki continued calling me every night, often crying, making me feel guilty, begging me to stay with her, telling me, "I need this." She would accuse me of trying to pull away from her—"Why are you doing this to me? I love you so much; you have no idea." Here she was, an adult in her forties with grown kids, and she was leaning on me, a twenty-one-year-old college student, for support, bawling on the phone that I was somehow betraying her.

Eventually, they accepted that I didn't want to have sex anymore, but they both insisted that I continue an emotional connection with Becki. A new routine began where she would text me every morning saying, "Good morning, gorgeous"; I would text her every night and say, "You're beautiful," or words to that effect. We texted back and forth throughout the day—random photos or a running commentary on the day's events, just checking in.

We still talked on the phone every night for an hour, regardless of what was going on in my life, and I would always say "I love you" before we hung up. At times, I would hear what sounded like typing—the soft clatter of a keyboard in the background. I finally asked Becki about it and she said, "Yeah, I'm taking notes." I have no idea what her motivation was, but I believe that every single phone conversation we had beyond a certain point in our relationship was documented. That added another worry to a growing pile.

Meanwhile, I struggled to keep the bulk of this a secret

from my new significant other. I was not only navigating a genuine relationship for the first time with a woman I cared about, but I also had to pretend all of this Becki stuff wasn't illicit or furtive. And the more I kept it hidden, the more illicit it became. It got so bad that Becki and I had a code word— "DT," which stood for "Don't Text"—whenever someone else was around.

If I tried to slack off or tend to my own life, or didn't get back to her quickly enough, there would be another guilt trip from Becki for trying to pull away from her. Then Jerry would have to get involved. He would text me separately and pressure me into maintaining the relationship. He'd say, "Becki mentioned you," or "A certain someone misses you . . . You should apologize for making her cry."

To draw me in closer, they also encouraged me to transfer to Liberty University and finish my degree there. Or maybe I could get my master's degree at Liberty after I wrapped up at Miami Dade. They suggested I move to Lynchburg and get involved in the family business. "Imagine living in Virginia; it would be so nice . . . You'd do so well up here. You'd rise up, you'd be able to buy a house. It's more affordable." A constant barrage of this, a relentless brainwashing that fed on my desire to better myself. I had planned to transfer to Florida State University or the University of Florida at some point, but this seemed like a stretch. There are still days when I wonder, *Imagine if I had gone that route; I'd be a senior executive at Liberty University right now. I could have avoided all this mess.* But of course, what they were proposing amounted to a form of indentured servitude.

In subsequent conversations, not all at once, I told Becki how I really felt, and without holding back: That the relationship was toxic and was damaging me psychologically. That I was anxious all the time. That I felt beholden to them, with the mandatory calls and constant texting; guilt trips when I tried to stop; serving as her emotional punching bag; and being forced to lie to my family and friends. And that it was weird to me how they went out of their way to befriend my family, which they did aggressively, even if on the surface it seemed admirable.

With the benefit of hindsight, I believe Jerry and Becki were grooming me from the very start. Every interaction was calculated. This is what con artists do. Letting me in on secrets that no one should know. Revealing how things really work beneath the surface. Making me feel like I was part of their inner circle. That's how they reeled me in. And in the moment I failed to realize what was happening to me. It was more than a little intoxicating. With Olivia, they probably considered it one more challenge, to pry me away from her, or sabotage the relationship in the hopes I'd come back to them. They were playing the long game, always. So I did what they asked, and texted with Becki to get her through the day, and called her to tuck her into bed at night, and tried to pay more attention to her when Jerry asked me to. I can't really say why I did it, other than they knew the right buttons to push, and it seemed the least destructive path forward. But it was exhausting.

The galling part is that falling into a trap like this is so out of character for me. I analyze everything. It's what they liked about me—or Jerry at least. And while he was praising me for my critical insights, a hand on my back, staring into the abyss of my future, it only took the slightest push to send me over the edge. He would just have to remind me that we had business between us, and how it would make things go more smoothly if we all stayed friends. He hung it over my head, insinuating to me, not all that subtly, where I'd be without them in my life.

And yet, on the business front, everything seemed to be going full steam ahead.

CHAPTER 7

BLIND TRUST

After our stay at the Gansevoort, I took Jerry at his word and started looking for property in South Beach and adjacent downtown areas. I called my sister and told her this couple who picked me up now wanted to go into business with me, and she told me to go for it. However it played out, it would still be a great hands-on opportunity to learn the business. Initially, I drove around aimlessly—downtown Miami, midtown, Doral, Wynwood, Little Havana, Coral Gables, Coconut Grove, and Miami Beach. I didn't use the published real estate listings; I just went by feel, exploring wherever my instincts led me. Later, my sister joined me and provided some tips.

Eventually I decided I needed to work with a real estate

agent to narrow down my search. I had a friend named Jesus Fernandez Jr., who I knew as Tito, who I met at Miami Dade. We all went out pub-crawling pretty regularly, and I came to understand that his father, Jesus Fernandez Sr., was a real estate broker who had been involved in some major deals, like flipping million-dollar houses. He also had his own real estate broker-age firm, Doral Isles Real Estate, that brokered residential and commercial properties. More recently, he seemed to have fallen on hard times. When I first met Tito and his father, they were living in an 8,000-square-foot mansion in Pinecrest, an upscale suburb of Miami comparable to Coral Gables. It was common at the time to have these grand homes for show, and then re-finance them to buy and sell smaller residential properties (or exotic cars and yachts). Come the financial meltdown of 2008, there were no more residents, and the whole thing came crash-ing down. Now, four years on, there weren't many real estate brokers still standing that hadn't at least gotten their hair singed. I knew Fernandez Sr. would know his way around a deal of this magnitude, and in the back of my mind, I thought this might be a way for their family to get back on their feet. As a business strategy—admittedly not yet fully formed—I was looking for win-win situations, and this seemed like an obvious one.

I reached out to Tito and told him I had investors who wanted to buy property and were willing to give me equity. If we closed on a deal, Tito would earn a commission on the sale. If it worked out, then maybe it could become an ongoing business model. Then I spoke to his dad. It was all very transparent. After some discussions, they were in, and Fernandez Sr. suggested he bring in another real estate broker named Luigi Gallegos, who was a former employee of Doral Isles and who still had his real estate license. They would all split the commission, so the number of brokers didn't matter to me.

There were some red flags from the beginning. Tito was charismatic and very funny, usually the life of the party, but he also had a big mouth. There were lots of times when we were out at the bars and he did something stupid and got us into trouble. Still, this was Miami. Everybody there had seen *Scarface* a hundred times, same as me. Going off in a nightclub was a rite of passage. These things were bound to happen, they just seemed to happen to Tito more often than most.

Sometime in May 2012, Jerry and Becki informed me they would be in Miami on one of their semi-annual getaways. Although they routinely used the Liberty corporate jet to fly down for mini-vacations like the one at the Fontainebleau when I'd met them (on the pretext of Jerry's "annual physical"), this time they flew commercial. I picked them up at the airport. I decided to use this opportunity to assemble the members of our team to make sure we were all on the same page. They were staying at the Loews Hotel in South Beach, as per usual, so I brought the Fernandezes to meet Jerry for drinks in the hotel bar.

We explained to Jerry we were looking for something with a hostel component. Tito worked at a hostel, and I argued that it could provide an income stream while we developed the property. It's a bare-bones business, simple to scale up or down. Real estate development often entails finding a distressed property and renovating it. In a target-rich environment like Miami and its surroundings, I thought that was our best bet, especially if I oversaw the renovations as a managing partner. I had seen my family do as much with the residential property in Mexico City, not to mention the apartment building my parents had inherited, and I had come to think of it as the family business. The conversation leaned mainly toward investment strategies and the improving state of the economy, and everyone pitched in ideas. After the meeting, the Fernandezes and their real estate agent got busy compiling a list of properties that met the criteria we had all agreed on. To the best of my knowledge, this was also the only time Tito ever met Jerry, though he claimed otherwise once the story had evolved.

In late June, Jerry and Becki returned with Chris Doyle, a vice president at CBRE (Coldwell Banker Richard Ellis, currently the largest commercial real estate services company in the world) and Jerry's frequent business partner in real estate acquisitions. Fernandez Sr. drove all of us around in his rental car while Doyle rode shotgun and I sat with Jerry in back. We looked at a number of properties they had highlighted, including some we liked but that came with historic preservation status. I'm all for the preservation of buildings, but it adds costs and severely limits what you can do with the property, which would have been a bureaucratic nightmare on our maiden voyage.

Afterward, we went to see Gallegos, the senior Fernandez's real estate agent. He had a second list of properties in the $5 million range for us to recon in the afternoon. In between, we had lunch at Puerto Sagua, a hole-in-the-wall Cuban joint on Collins Avenue that you'd have to be a local to know about, and Gallegos joined us. The group (without Tito, it's worth noting) seemed to have an easy rapport, and although their styles were different, the Lynchburg contingent seemed to mesh easily with the Miami high rollers (or former high rollers) I had brought on board.

I had class that evening, so the team dropped me off and then went to check out the last entry on the list, a high-volume hostel business at 810 Alton Road that catered to backpackers and spring breakers, with decent ratings on Tripadvisor and various travel sites. Located in a mainly residential area, the hostel was insulated from the tourist traffic of South Beach, making for calmer and less chaotic surroundings.

After I left a lecture that had been extremely difficult to focus on, Jerry called to report on the last property on their list. "We really love it," he said. "It looks really good." I drove back and looked at it that night, and when I did my own research the next day, I got really excited as well. The asking price was $5 million on the nose.

Up to that point, Chris Doyle was a potential partner in the property, with the purchase going through Comeback Inn, LLC, a company that he and Jerry had used before to purchase commercial real estate. (Politico has identified Trey Falwell as a silent partner.) The name comes from a run-down abandoned hotel in Lynchburg they had purchased and successfully transformed into the local La Quinta franchise, so presumably the parameters of the Alton Road deal would have appealed to him. I spent a fair amount of time talking with Chris about the business, and how we might cut expenses, which was his magic bullet for making real estate ventures pay off. Ultimately, he thought the asking price was too high and decided the deal was too rich for his blood, and he pulled out, which was fine by me. The property was ultimately purchased through Alton Hostel, LLC. I also thought the price was inflated, but given the three cardinal rules of real estate investment ("location, location, location"), it couldn't help but appreciate in value. It was zoned for six stories, but only had two floors at present, meaning the real value was in redevelopment; it was mixed-use, with street-level retail of an

Italian restaurant and a liquor store and topped by apartments with paying tenants; plus there were similar investments taking place all around it. Whatever money we put into it now would only enhance the value.

The Falwells returned to Miami in August for a vacation and so Jerry, along with Trey, could meet with the seller. I went with them. Joe Comesana was a Cuban exile who had left the island in 1961, the same as my father, relocating first to New York and later Miami Beach. We met at Hotel 18, another one of his properties, and he and I fell into a discussion of pre-Castro Cuba, and I gave him a rundown of my family's history there, which served as an icebreaker. Afterward, he was comfortable enough to walk us through his accounting records so we could see the true value of the property and the business, all of which looked good.

But soon after we entered into negotiations to buy the building, Tito began making increasingly outrageous demands for money he said he was due. The terms were spelled out explicitly from the very beginning. I have no idea how much they ultimately were promised for their commission, because I considered the matter something between Jerry, Gallegos, and the Fernandezes. Except for Tito, I figured they were all experienced in real estate transactions of this size and scale, and could certainly look out for their own interests. Nevertheless, as the closing date approached, Tito's demands trudged steadily northward. Eventually, he demanded an equity stake, same as me, which I painstakingly explained to him was not part of our original deal. He maintained he had helped create the financial projections, where you look at a property and measure the size, specs, estimated expenses, prospective revenue and taxes, put it on an Excel spreadsheet, and then determine a valuation. There are people like Jerry who can eyeball it and get pretty close on the back of a cocktail napkin.

In this case, Jerry asked his son Trey and me to come up with the preliminary version as a learning exercise, with Chris Doyle checking our work. In no universe would Tito have been involved in those calculations, because he had no specific financial expertise. And yet here he was claiming that he was being taken advantage of, and becoming increasingly agitated and aggressive. I alerted Jerry to what was happening, and he told me, "Dealing with people with conflicting agendas is the hardest thing about business. You just need to be firm and power through."

Eventually, I had to break off all communications with Tito, as he was constantly trying to strongarm me. He wasn't able to manage his emotions, and he was becoming a loose cannon. I could see it was time to cut my losses. From then on, all my communications went through his father, who appeared much more calm, logical, and easy to deal with. Fernandez Sr. told me, "Are we gonna finish this deal? Are we gonna close it? Then we're good."

Then began the due diligence period, which is a substantial undertaking: You have to survey the property, conduct environmental and soil studies, get an appraisal, and provide easements, encumbrances, recent tax bills, zoning documents, as-built construction documents, previous site plans, material correspondence related to the property—all kinds of things. That takes time, usually several months, and with attorney fees and other costs, can be very expensive—maybe as much as $100,000.

In my dealings with Fernandez Sr. in the run-up to the closing, I could see the same sort of arguments and attitude in the father as I had the son. At one point, he made a cryptic remark to me, something like, "I've got a friend who has a picture or two. What are you going to do when they start knocking on your door?" I had no idea what he was talking about. I had been very careful to conceal the nature of my relationship with Becki. And besides, the affair was over with (or so I thought at the time). This was business. Did he mean the paparazzi would see us out at dinner together and get suspicious? His comment sounded heartfelt, and yet it could also read as a threat. Maybe he was fishing. I told Jerry he was becoming a problem, and I think Jerry may have called him, which apparently did the trick. Once we closed and the Fernandezes got their money, we no longer had to deal with them. Good riddance.

Despite my warning about the Fernandezes, Jerry and Becki didn't take it seriously. They said I was being paranoid. "No one's psychic," they would tell me. "They don't know our business." They had a lot more experience than me, but I thought they were being incredibly naive. I'd say, "You guys don't understand how Miami works. People are sharks here, same as they are in New York. You go out to dinner and people know who you are, people hear you discussing various topics, they figure stuff out. It's not like Lynchburg where you own everything."

But they seemed to have bigger things on their minds. I had no idea just how big.

CHAPTER 8

CITY OF THE SEVEN HILLS

In early September 2012, I received an email from Becki inviting me to a special event at Liberty University: Donald Trump, then publicly contemplating a presidential run, had been invited to speak at the university's twice-weekly Convocation on September 24. Convocation is a gathering where Liberty students listen to various dignitaries and bellwethers from the fundamentalist Christian ecosystem, and attendance was mandatory, assuring a ready-made, sympathetic audience. Past speakers include a who's who of evangelical politics and conservative culture: George H. W. Bush, Jeb Bush, Ted Cruz, Mitt Romney, Jordan Peterson, Laura Ingraham, Glenn Beck, Mel Gibson, Randall Wallace (the screenwriter of *Braveheart*), actor Vince

Vaughn, Willie Robertson from *Duck Dynasty* (the Falwells were friends with the whole Robertson clan), Pattie Mallette (Justin Bieber's mom), Michele Bachmann, Fox News host Shannon Bream, Ben Carson, and Jimmy Carter, among many others. Bernie Sanders famously spoke there in September 2015; a Liberty source told me that students were instructed to be on their best behavior, lest the university appear to be less than gracious.

Although Liberty University was officially a nonprofit institution, and therefore politically agnostic, it was widely considered a flagship of the Christian right, and any conservative politician seeking the presidency would have to come and kiss the ring. And since Jerry currently wore the ring, this was his and Becki's moment to bask in the light. They invited me to fly up as their guest, stay at the family compound, and attend the event, including an exclusive luncheon for twenty-five on the last day. I was included with the family—right below their son Wesley and daughter Caroline—on the guest list circulated to attendees. I didn't invite Olivia. I was vague about the circumstances, telling her it was "a business trip"—something I felt bad about at the time and am still ashamed of. There's a photo of me aboard the Liberty jet from that weekend, but that was just me aspiring to the life of luxury (one Instagram photo at a time). I actually flew commercial on my own dime. (The luncheon was ultimately canceled because Trump was running late.)

At the time, my politics were similar to Becki and Jerry's. I grew up Republican, in a conventionally conservative subculture, and I believed in personal liberty: I was pro-business, pro-capitalism, and pro–making as much money as you can legally and ethically. I believe that Jerry had a master plan to ease out of Liberty eventually, possibly pass the torch to his brother, invest in real estate under his own banner, and create something epic he could call his own. I didn't have to be an evangelical zealot or a Christian nationalist to find common cause with that business vision. They saw my potential and how my energy, ambition, enthusiasm, and work ethic could help them achieve their goals, and I shared enough of their core beliefs to be an asset to them. On more than one occasion, hanging out, having drinks with his kids, Jerry would point in turn to Trey, Wesley, and me and say, "I want you and you and you . . . to create something."

Bringing me into their private domain at the exact moment of their political coronation, to meet my childhood hero no less, could go a long way toward cementing that future business relationship. They eventually introduced me as a surrogate member of the family, but really I was someone they could introduce to their inner circle—or maybe sell to their credulous followers—if they could only get past the initial optics.

I stayed with Becki and Jerry at their farm Thursday through Sunday. Their property is about six hundred acres, located in nearby Goode, Virginia, thirty minutes due west of Lynchburg. Although their house is often referred to in the press as a mansion, it's really not. It's a traditional southern colonial home with four or five bedrooms, including the guest room where I stayed (as well as a separate guesthouse that will figure into the story later on). The grounds are stunning: the legendary Blue Ridge Mountains framed in the distance, a massive man-made lake nearby where we went wakeboarding and rode Jet-Skis. We also did target shooting at milk jugs and Coke cans whenever we felt like it. I had a great time.

This was also my first time meeting the Falwell kids, all three of whom were present for this watershed event in the family's history. They had been told that their parents were going into business with me (and I was already technically in business with Trey, as per his father's wishes), that I'd had a tough life, but was a bright kid, and they wanted to set me up for success. This all seemed plausible enough at the time. Or at least it didn't seem patently absurd. It was on that trip that Becki began referring to Trey and Wesley as my brothers. Trey was a couple of years older than me and I think had his own place by then, and Wesley was a year younger and still lived at home. Trey had graduated from Liberty with (I believe) a business degree. He managed his family's properties before I met them, and at his parents' behest would go on to manage a portion of the real estate portfolio for Liberty University through his management company. (He was also employed by the university as vice president of operations.) The whole time I knew him, he seemed bloodless—cold, unnecessarily rude (cruel, even)—especially to Becki and his girlfriend (later his wife). He generally rose above the fray when tempers were running hot, but rarely engaged emotionally with the family. Jerry found his behavior inexplicable and often said he didn't know who Trey got his personality from. "I don't know how he came out like that," he joked to me more than once. He was not a pleasant person to be around.

Wesley was more like a normal college student or laid-back party guy. He didn't seem particularly interested in school or the family business. He played guitar, drums, and several other instruments: at some point, he took up the handpan, a spherical metal drum whose surface produces different tones, and discovered that he really liked working with his hands. This led him to the welding department at Liberty, where he quickly rose to a managing role. He was a good kid and fun to hang out with, essentially a hippie who Jerry said reminded him of himself when he was younger. (Wes eventually joined his brother five or six years later in managing the family-owned properties.) I also met Caroline on that trip. She seemed both sweet and lovely, but at barely twelve, she was really too young for me ever to get a handle on her personality, then or later.

When we went out in public, and as more and more people arrived throughout the weekend, Jerry and Becki introduced me as a friend of Trey's and their potential business partner, and Trey seemed fine with that. Their standard line became their sons "needed a friend outside the bubble," which was admirable, if not exactly true.

My first night at their house, Becki and Jerry tried to coax me into one of our sexcapades, but I reiterated I was with someone else now and they needed to respect my boundaries, and after a little while they did. Jerry confided to me, "You know, we're not going to tell Olivia if you don't," but when I didn't take the bait, they let it drop. I told them I'd rather focus on us being friends and potential business partners right now, and they seemed to accept that.

Up to that point, they were both fairly easygoing, each in their own way: Becki was vivacious and young at heart—maybe more so than practically anyone else her age. She was still obsessed, and at times distraught, which her husband either tolerated or got off on, leaving me to try and be the adult in the situation. But really, what did I know about it? Maybe this was simply how grown-ups coped with sex stuff, in and outside of a relationship. Jerry, at least once he had a few drinks in him, was generally affable and floated above it all; their drinking tended to take the edge off. We had a good vibe between us. Even their kids commented on it.

That weekend, though, is when I first began to see things more clearly through this haze. Early in the weekend, the three of us went out to shoot guns on their property. Afterward, we were in the kitchen making drinks—Becki vodka, Jerry and me tequila—and Jerry made one of his veiled jokes, the kind that carried a tinge of menace.

He said, "If Becki were to ever run off with someone—now I know who it would be. And if that were to happen, if she ever tried to divorce me, well . . . I suppose I'd have to kill you." He smiled as he said it, and so did Becki. But his meaning seemed clear enough to me. He may have chosen this moment to say it—surrounded by wealth, and just over the hill from the unbridled power he wielded—to make the point that he could probably get away with it. Here are two of the most powerful people in the state, if not the country, and I'm on their private property, with gunshot residue all over my hands and my fingerprints all over their guns. There's poor cellular service and a spotty Wi-Fi signal up at the big house, and the local constabulary acts as their honor guard and private security detail. They're on a texting basis with the sheriff. I tried not to let my imagination run wild, but they could bury me in the south forty without a trace.

I was doing my level best to get Becki back to a low boil and make it all seem innocuous enough to my new girlfriend, while closing a multimillion-dollar business deal I believed I might never get this close to again, and now I had to worry about this?

Spending time in Lynchburg, it was clear Jerry Falwell Sr. still exerted a huge influence at Liberty and throughout the evangelical community. On his sudden death in 2007, Jerry Jr. assumed the presidency at Liberty while his brother, Jonathan, took over the pulpit at the Thomas Road Baptist megachurch. But Jerry wasn't the only one descended from local royalty. Becki's father, Thomas E. Tilley, presided over a $20 million real estate and mobile home empire in North Carolina, and partially financed construction of the Tilley Center on campus, which was named for him. Becki claimed she grew up "poor," since her family's assets produced relatively little cash. But that strikes me as a cover story she used to disarm people when their lifestyle seemed jarring in light of Liberty's nonprofit status. In 2002, Tilley sued the IRS to recover back taxes paid in the early nineties. And in 2015, at eighty years old, he was sentenced to thirty-six months in prison, minus time served, and ordered to pay $7,675,000 in restitution to the IRS for income tax fraud dating back to at least 1993. According to a Justice Department statement, as recently as 2009, he had claimed an annual income of $822,000 and a net worth of $30 million. In the words of Tom Arnold, who will enter the story shortly, "They're all a bunch of grifters."

But you wouldn't know it from a leisurely stroll around the grounds of Liberty University. Nonprofit or not, Liberty was the family business and they were its founding family. Becki and Jerry met when she was thirteen and he was sixteen, and they started dating five years later, once Becki turned eighteen. In retrospect, their subsequent union and the commingling of the family fortunes seems as preordained as the marriages between European monarchies. As we toured the campus's manicured lawns and impeccable landscaping, the students who noticed the Falwells acted like they'd suddenly encountered the Beatles strolling unaccompanied on Abbey Road. A pocket of them would gather, then part like the Red Sea for us to pass, and then the whole thing would happen all over again.

The Falwells handpicked Liberty's board, cowed the administration, and leaned heavily on the scales to get their way. They absolutely derived the benefits, too—not only the salary, but rampant nepotism, sweetheart deals, and rubbing elbows with the power elite, like Donald Trump. Based on my first impression, Liberty was one big playground for them. I also think it was Becki who was the brains of the operation. Jerry has a good head for business, but he's socially awkward and basically a goofball. It was Becki who cultivated the political connections and had the vision. She has the charisma, innate charm, and above-average emotional intelligence to ingratiate herself to those more powerful. And her social graces nurtured Jerry's connections through phone calls and emails. I saw it in how Trump responded to the two of them. If he was the heir to the dynasty in name, then she was the power behind the throne.

But all of this, the veiled threats, family dynamics, and illicit agendas, receded into the background the second the circus hit town.

Donald Trump was coming to Lynchburg.

CHAPTER 9

THE ELEPHANT IN THE ROOM

There's the widespread perception that Jerry Falwell Jr., for all his business savvy and success in the real estate market—not to mention having single-handedly rescued Liberty from its financial death spiral—was agnostic toward the religious tenets on which the family business was founded. It was his brother, Jonathan, who was the religious one, now the pastor at Thomas Road Baptist Church, where Jerry Sr. had made the Falwell name.

The Falwell family history could not be more colorful. Jerry Sr.'s father, Carey Falwell, ran the local bus line, and his two brothers Garland and Warren ran their own gas station and restaurant, respectively, outside the city limits. But their main livelihood came from being Lynchburg's biggest bootleggers, supplying moonshine to the local brothels and "nip joints," those speakeasies in a roadside shack that saw the locals through Prohibition. Eventually, Carey shot and killed Garland in an alcohol-fueled brawl, then slowly drank himself to death over the ensuing decade and a half.

Jerry Sr. founded Thomas Road in 1956 at the age of twenty-two and remained its pastor until his death in 2007, an astounding fifty years in the pulpit. Initially, he presented a welcome alternative to the fire-and-brimstone preachers who found sin and perdition around every corner. Falwell's delivery, by contrast, was affable, homespun, courtly even, which played well to the intimacy of television. He briefly considered a run for elected office, using his televised sermons as a springboard, but ultimately it proved easier to bring politics to the pulpit than the Bible to the statehouse. Despite his folksy demeanor, though, Falwell was a fierce advocate of "religious freedom," a rallying cry among mostly southern religious universities opposing the tide of civil rights legislation just then sweeping through American institutions. This culminated in his founding the Moral Majority in 1979 with arch-conservative activist Paul Weyrich, which a year later was widely credited with electing Ronald Reagan and energizing the evangelical right.

No stranger to controversy, Falwell met with a public reckoning of sorts the day after the 9/11 attacks, in an interview with Pat Robertson on *The 700 Club* in which he said, "The abortionists have got to bear some burden for this because God will not be mocked. And when we destroy forty million little innocent babies, we make God mad. I really believe that the pagans, and the abortionists, and the feminists, and the gays and the lesbians who are actively trying to make that an alternative lifestyle, the ACLU, People for the American Way, all of them who have tried to secularize America, I point the finger in their face and say, 'You helped this happen.' " Reaction was swift, and Falwell was forced to recant a day later, claiming his remarks had been taken out of context after President Bush called them "inappropriate." But that template—toeing the line of acceptable political discourse in order to drag the national debate steadily to the right—made him a kingmaker inside the partisan bubble he had helped create, and ultimately grew into another hallmark of their makeshift dynasty. And Liberty was its proof of concept, a magic kingdom where such impolitic ideas could roam free and unfettered.

Up until his death, Falwell Sr. routinely addressed the Liberty student body with one of his stock quotes, how if the campus should ever fall under the sway of the liberals, those in attendance should return to their alma mater and burn it to the ground. As late as 2017, Jonathan Falwell revived a version of the quote, promising to personally "light the match."

As religious affiliation in America shrinks, the percentage who are evangelicals expands steadily. And in 2016, four-fifths of white evangelicals would vote for Donald Trump. It's easy to see why in September 2012, at the height of Obama's reelection campaign, Trump would set his sights on coming to Lynchburg.

People come to speak at the Convocation first because it's an honor, this being a flagship of evangelical conservatism, and second because they may have an agenda they're promoting. Politicians are frequent guests, their agenda usually being themselves. Donald Trump spoke about his path from childhood to successful real estate developer, how to handle pressure, and his perception of our economy and failed foreign policy.

Before Trump arrived, the Liberty grounds were crawling with security personnel and what I assumed to be Secret Service agents (although at that point, they were probably just hired security), the media train that was already following him around, plus the local press. I waited in the green room backstage at the Vines Center, the sports arena where the Convocation was held, as over ten thousand students and their guests filled the main hall. It was there I met the former congresswoman Michele Bachmann, a Tea Party founder and 2012 Republican presidential candidate, and her daughter. She kept asking me how I knew the Falwells. I knew who she was, so I kept it vague.

And then Jerry arrived with Trump and his entourage. Trump had some beauty pageant girls with him; one had been Miss Virginia or something in the Miss Universe pageant and had graduated from Liberty. He's a large man, six foot three, and physically imposing—250 pounds, give or take. Jerry beamed as he introduced me as a friend of theirs from Miami who he was mentoring, "our friend from the Fontainebleau."

Trump lit up at the mention. "Oh, the Fontainebleau? I love the Fontainebleau. A lot of my friends from Mar-a-Lago go there. Love it, love it, love it." Trump has a way of focusing intently on you when he's talking to you—maybe all famous people do that. But he's so big that he winds up peering down at most people like a large bird of prey. Jerry told him I was going to be their business partner in a commercial property in South Beach, which made me a fellow real estate impresario—as it did Jerry. I was clearly starstruck. Trump was charming for the entirety of our interaction, which lasted all of thirty seconds, and not like he was portrayed on television.

There's a picture of us taken at the exact instant we shook

hands, and you can see Becki on the left behind him, her eyes laser-focused on me, like I was a debutante at a cotillion and she was the proud society matron. I asked Trump to sign my well-worn copy of *The Art of the Deal* and he wrote, "Giancarlo, work hard."

After everyone had their Trump moment and the photographers were sated, we were ushered into a closed room where media weren't allowed: me, Jerry and Becki, their three kids, Trump, and a dour-looking guy in an expensive suit with salt-and-pepper hair who didn't say anything but looked like he didn't miss much. I later found out he was Trump's fixer, Michael Cohen. We were in there maybe ten minutes, during which time Jerry and Trump talked politics and the rest of us listened intently. Jerry brought up climate change and how he thought it was a hoax, how it wasn't good for business, a conspiracy theory to make the people selling it get rich. Trump mostly let Jerry talk, occasionally nodding with a grave expression to validate what Jerry was saying.

And then they were ready for us in the main auditorium. Before Trump was introduced, but after everyone else had taken their seats, they seated the Falwell family in the front row with me in tow. The place was packed, and they showed us on the giant jumbotron screen, like at Yankee Stadium or something. The Falwells were like the British royal family, with the assembled crowd following their every movement. The whole time walking to our seats, I had to remember to monitor my breathing and try not to trip. It was surreal.

Jerry led the Convocation. He is not a natural public speaker like his father or brother, Jonathan. He's more like the CEO of a successful company who has to address a shareholders meeting and can deliver his talking points and manage a decent Power-Point presentation. When he was preparing his introduction he asked me to tell him interesting details from Trump's book *The Art of the Deal*, since he knew I had read it multiple times and committed large parts to memory. We went over the various deals, and I told him the story of Trump punching his second-grade teacher, which Jerry cited in a Q&A with Trump after his speech. The speech Trump gave would be familiar in tone and substance to anyone listening today. At one point he told the auditorium of college students, "Make sure you get a prenup." He didn't seem like a natural fit with this audience, but he was sowing seeds for his eventual return in 2016 when he was formally on the campaign trail.

After the Convocation, we all took a walking tour of the campus. As usual, everywhere we went, Jerry and Becki were treated like royalty. After that, we were supposed to have our private dinner with the exclusive guest list, but they announced Trump was running late for his flight, and he and his entourage sped off in a caravan of Suburbans to their next would-be campaign stop.

One thing that stayed with me from that day above everything else: During our tour, I was walking behind Michael Cohen (although I didn't know his name yet), who was talking with Chris Doyle. At one point, Cohen looked back at me, and then I heard him ask, "Who is that guy?" Doyle whispered something I couldn't hear, and then Cohen said, "Huh," like he was making a mental note of it.

Spending time on campus, I saw a side of the Falwells I hadn't seen up to that point. Everything seemed unreal there—cosmetically perfect, but artificial, lacking any vitality of real life.

The engine of social control over the student body is its elaborate and punitive honor code, called the Liberty Way, which demands that students refrain not only from premarital sex and traditional college vices like drinking and smoking, but also using profane language and being alone with a member of the opposite sex, particularly at off-campus residences. It's safe to say these guidelines do not extend to upper-level management. Perusing the Liberty Way code, I was struck by how the focus on sex seemed mostly a way to control women. They're the ones who have to deal with the potential fallout from having sex—whether pregnancy, damage to their reputation, or sexual violence. They are also the easiest to identify as having transgressed, so they become the easiest to punish. The onus is on women to conform in a way it's not for their male counterparts.

The students I met on campus all had a searching quality—a certain credulousness and eagerness to please. Everyone seemed happy, pleasant, often exuberant (having just encountered the First Couple in their natural habitat). But there was also something missing, which was harder to identify. Certainly the campus was beautiful, with its billion-dollar face-lift that Jerry had engineered. Maybe they disappeared into the background too easily; they were shiny in the same way, reflected the light at the same angles, and as such the people were indistinguishable from the landscape.

In this way, they were like me. Meaning that whatever the Falwells recognized in me that made me an easy mark, the same quality was present in everyone I met there, probably selected by some feature that was built into the system. These students were there because their parents wanted them to be there. It was safe—statistically so; it served as a redoubt from the secular world; it was a private Eden for people of like minds to congregate and celebrate their shared ideals. And if there were lingering doubts, they had each other as all the evidence they needed.

Which is why it was so disconcerting to watch a ten-minute promotional video for Liberty University that Becki had alerted me to before I arrived. Titled *Thank You, Becki and Jerry*, and produced by Devin Olson Media in 2010, it perfectly captures Becki and Jerry's self-image as the golden couple within the insular world of Liberty University, and the fun parents all the students gravitated toward. Bushy-tailed students scattered about the university grounds attest to the couple's perceived virtues, falling over themselves to pay tribute to their beloved leaders.

"One of the main things that I personally notice as a student, from Jerry and Becki, is their marriage bonds them as leadership in Liberty," says a Woman Reclining in the Grass at the five-minute mark. "And for me to see that, and for me to see their family, and how welcoming they are to the student body, as far as senior picnics and holding events at their house and inviting people over—that has spoken to me . . ."

"I really appreciate you for just being personal with the students and getting down on our level, and not being some high-and-mighty leaders," she adds in a second clip.

"A lot of people say she's like a mom," says the Guy in a Red Shirt two minutes later. "She's fun to hug, she's always got a smile on her face, and she's usually got a camera in her hand—so expect a picture to be taken at some point."

At least one of those pictures Becki took was a shirtless photo of Ben Crosswhite, Becki and Jerry's personal trainer. She showed it to me on numerous occasions, I thought possibly to try and make me jealous. Ben reminded me of . . . me—if I had stayed within the fold. With Jerry's guidance, Ben bought a training gym from Liberty valued at $1.2 million for no money down, then leased the tennis courts back to the university for $650,000 over eight years, and financed it all at 3 percent interest.

It's worth noting that after my story went public, casting a bright light on all of the Falwells' sub-rosa relationships, Ben claimed he had purchased the property at fair market value—done them a favor, really, since it had been a huge financial drain on Liberty's bottom line. To make his point, he sued Reuters news agency, which first reported the details of the transaction a year and a half earlier. (The suit was dismissed as untimely.)

His career arc, meteoric and charmed, made me wonder whether he had a similar relationship with the Falwells as mine. He looked like how you would imagine a professional trainer would look; whenever I was around him he was relentlessly positive and upbeat; and beneath it all he seemed very ambitious.

Much later, in 2018, after everything had gotten weird, I recorded a phone call with Becki. It was my response to her incessant note-taking, and it's something I did on occasion. In the brief snippet, which runs thirty-four seconds, Becki sounds a little tipsy as she confronts the rumors she has heard, including the ones about her and Ben Crosswhite.

Playing devil's advocate, I said, "Well, Ben Crosswhite did send you a shirtless picture in a towel."

"Oh gosh," Becki said. " 'Cause he's frickin' gay. He sent it to Jerry too."

"No he's not," I said, pushing back. "He's married."

"*He's not gay*," she said, making fun of my naivete. "Uh-huh. He hits Jerry on the butt more than he hits me on the butt."

To be clear, Ben *is* married, so I'm casting no aspersions. Becki's comeback could just as easily have been to quell the rumors or to win an argument, and to take Ben out of the running in any list of her potential suitors. But I did remember seeing the same photo on Jerry's phone. He may have even showed it to me. He was not shy about sharing inappropriate screenshots with anyone who seemed interested.

Heck, Jerry was known to send questionable photos to lots of people, including board members. He often pointed out how hot his wife was, or bragged about his own prowess. At the May 2019 Liberty commencement, the one where Vice President Pence delivered the keynote address, Jerry introduced Becki, wearing an orange Liberty Flames dress he had bought her, by saying, "I think it's very fitting that she's wearing that dress, because I believe she's the hottest First Lady at any college in the country."

Anyway, as Jerry never tired of telling me, especially in regards to our own curious arrangement, "I don't have a gay bone in my body." So, who knows?

As soon as I returned to Miami, I gave notice at the Fontainebleau. While it had been fun—I met some cool people and it managed to break me out of my shell once and for all—it was also a brutal and taxing job. I had saved enough money to attend college full-time and was ready for the next stage of my life. The general manager tried to talk me out of it. He told me the guys above him all made $250,000, and I would be a shoo-in for management track. I can still remember his parting words when I stopped by to pick up my last paycheck:

"You shouldn't do it, man. Wise up here."

CHAPTER 10

HOSTEL TAKEOVER

I left work in October. If memory serves, we closed on the Miami Beach property on February 23, 2013, Becki's forty-eighth birthday. The percentages were all spelled out from the outset so that there would be no confusion. Jerry would secure the money, with 80 percent of the purchase price coming from financing. Jerry and Becki would own 50 percent (under Becki's name) and Trey and I would each own 25 percent, although in the end, I accepted 24.9 percent, with Becki receiving the additional .1 percent (which presumably gave them veto power). In lieu of putting up cash, I would manage the business until such time as we could develop or flip the property. Jerry had estimated the real estate as worth $3 million and the business another $1.8 million. Of that $4.8 million purchase price, he paid $4.65 million through a 4.5 percent interest loan with a twenty-year amortization, and the balance escrowed toward outstanding deal points that were eventually resolved. As I understood it, Jerry provided the down payment himself, although his name showed up nowhere on the deed or in the purchase documents. He also requested that both buyer and seller be kept confidential. Becki (as Rebecca) was listed as a member of the corporation.

I now owned a 25 percent share in a multimillion-dollar property. Forget the mortgage and my partners and whatever I stood to pocket if I cashed out. Especially forget the salary I'd be working for in lieu of my share of the investment, $276 a week, which I would have to make up for from my savings. (Property managers routinely make between $40,000 and $50,000 annually, plus bonuses.) After the closing, Gallegos asked to meet with me and gave me an envelope with $5,000 cash in it, which he called a finder's fee. This is not uncommon in the industry, and I was encouraged to write it off as an incentive or best practice. Like the Fernandezes, he moved on after the closing.

I was told Gallegos was suffering from a chronic illness—so much so that he couldn't fill out the relevant paperwork, and his wife had to receive his commission. It was only much later that I learned he had been indicted on charges of grand theft, first degree, which means theft in the amount of $100,000 or greater, punishable by up to thirty years in Florida state prison and a fine of up to $10,000. Gallegos was ultimately convicted, fined, and served a probationary term until his death in 2016 at the age of seventy-nine. He also had an IRS lien and at least one bankruptcy in his past that I had not been aware of.

With the deal behind us, Trey and I took over the day-today operations of the property. In addition to the hostel, MB Liquors, a storefront package store, pretty much took care of itself, and the on-site restaurant, Macchialina, however improbably, quickly became one the most popular Italian restaurants in Miami. Founded in June 2012 by Chef Michael Pirolo, it was named Best Restaurant in 2013 by *Miami New Times* and given an "excellent" rating by the *Miami Herald*. Three years later, Pirolo himself was a semifinalist for Best Chef South in the prestigious James Beard Awards for 2016, and is today recognized as one of Miami's top chefs and sommeliers. None of which we had anything to do with, but I'm still proud of it, and having a business like that on premises only enhanced our profile. Pirolo started at Scarpetta, a top-tier Italian restaurant in New York City, and was named executive chef of Scarpetta when it was franchised at the Fontainebleau. There's a back door at the hostel that leads to the Macchialina kitchen, and I would often pop over for a quick lunch, where we would bond over time at the famed Miami landmark. (Joe Comesana, who sold us the place, also stuck around for a couple of months to make sure we got on our feet, even though there was nothing contractually that said he had to.)

Miami Hostel was a high-volume business providing humble accommodations for between twenty and twenty-five dollars a night to college-age travelers and spring breakers more interested in spending their time on the beaches and in the bars. Hostels like ours, sleeping six to a room, with a common area big enough for a hundred of their peers, was a beachhead for everything guests come here for. Still, we always knew that redevelopment was the ultimate plan. My job was to maximize the value of the property by overseeing capital improvement projects and keep the cash flowing until we sold or launched into something bigger.

Trey was a good partner, in that I was free to handle the day-to-day responsibilities as I saw fit. The hostel business, which I oversaw, generated an estimated combined effective gross revenue of $838,000 annually. I probably oversaw another million dollars' worth of capital improvements during my time there. We dealt with attorneys, engineers, architects, painters, plumbers, suppliers—you name it. If we needed construction, I would automatically solicit three bids, negotiate each, get the best price and stay on top of it until the work was completed.

I developed a sense of when I was in the sweet spot with vendors and when things were getting too comfortable and the service would start slipping or I appeared ripe for the plucking. Jerry gave us free legal advice and served as an unofficial consultant, which saved us a fortune. When I moved to another city, I kept on top of everything remotely.

All in all, it was an easy job, since it was 100 percent problem-solving—either something breaks and you fix it, or else you isolate a solution to a persistent or systemic problem. Either way, lean into it and things get better. An audit estimated the property value at $7.9 million, and we received offers of between $6 and $7 million in 2015, 2016, and 2017, so I'm confident things were headed in the right direction under my stewardship. My guess is the property today is worth $10 million.

And just as we became the proud owners of a high-volume youth hostel in the boomtown of Miami Beach, a spate of articles in the press seemed to confirm our prescience and business acumen. An article in the *Miami Herald* in April 2013 reported that local hotels were up 5 percent in occupancy over the year before, March was "record-breaking," and the recession was resoundingly over.

"I think our timing on buying the hostel was perfect," Jerry emailed the group. "Your business judgment is very good, Gian!"

The Falwells liked to keep team spirit flowing with a mutually reaffirming email thread, so Becki chimed in with, "Amazing. That's why we fought so hard to get it closed in February. I told Jerry your idea of contacting hospitality schools [to] work out a deal to get students this summer. He thinks it's a great plan."

In 2014, we amended the articles of incorporation to change my role to that of a managing member. This enabled me to sign contracts, execute legal documents, et cetera, on behalf of Alton Hostel, LLC, since members (i.e., owners) don't have the authority to act as a manager. I was twenty-two at the time.

In August, the *Wall Street Journal* reported that a "new breed of hostels" was headed to the US. Perfected in the capitals of Europe, they were taking their cues from boutique hotels and catering to a younger, hipper clientele, all the things I had been drumming into them since I'd broached the concept. Deep-pocketed investors were targeting New York, DC, and San Francisco, and Miami couldn't be far behind. Even billionaire and Clinton crony Ron Burkle had taken the plunge with the Freehand Miami, a mere three miles north of us.

Our specific goal was to eventually redevelop the property as a six-story mixed-use residential site with street-level retail, which fit the area trend. Developer Russell Galbut and his mammoth Crescent Heights development company planned a 64,000-square-foot multilevel retail project to be named 700 Alton Road, essentially right next door to us at 810. His other company, GFO investments, planned a forty-eight-story condo tower at 500 Alton Road that would be the tallest building in Miami Beach. It's as if we had shot an arrow into the exact epicenter of the hot new commercial real estate market.

Liberty publicist Johnnie Moore had managed to place an article in the *Washington Post*, of all places—a borderline puff piece that ran in early March 2013. Under the headline "Virginia's Liberty Transforms into Evangelical Mega-University," author Nick Anderson credits "the online education boom" with doubling the university's head count twice over in the six years since its patriarch's demise. It liberally quotes Jerry as chancellor and president, framing the enterprise exactly as he pitched it—to be "for evangelical Christians what Notre Dame is for Catholics and Brigham Young is for Mormons"—and, more importantly, defining Jerry as the voice of reason compared to his father's polarizing demagogue. "We're not the Moral Majority anymore," they quote Jerry as saying. "We're not a church. Our mission is to educate." However anodyne, it was a formal introduction on the national stage that didn't frame Jerry in the shadow of his father. The Falwell clan was ecstatic, and the sense that they finally had turned a corner and were coming up in the world pervaded our business adventure as well.

AS I SETTLED INTO MY NEW POSITION, STILL TAKING CLASSES at Miami Dade, things were proceeding nicely with Olivia. And while Becki and I had hit the pause button on our illicit entanglements, she still played an outsize role in orchestrating my personal life. She and Jerry invited us out for dinner during one of their routine vacation weekends in Miami around the time of the closing. Learning that my new partner was on a premed track, Becki turned her attentions to securing Olivia a six-week rotational internship at one of the local hospitals in Lynchburg. Olivia was very grateful for Becki's kindness and took her up on it, moving to Lynchburg, where they had found an apartment for her. Which is how I came to visit her for two weeks in early July 2013 to celebrate our one-year anniversary. When it came time to leave, the Falwells happened to be heading down to Miami, too, and they offered me a ride on their private jet.

So Jerry; Trey and Wesley and their girlfriends (and future wives); Ben Crosswhite (their personal trainer); their nephew (who was also the pilot); a man nicknamed Big Ben, who takes care of the farm for them; and I all piled into Liberty's chartered corporate jet at Falwell Airport. All of us, that is, except for Becki, who we had to wait on as usual. She ran behind schedule so consistently her kids had T-shirts printed up that said, WHERE'S BECKI? This was the only time I traveled on their private jet. It was well-stocked with booze, and Jerry filled up his signature water bottle laced with tequila. It turns out Jerry was terrified of flying and talked incessantly to distract himself. At Becki's request, Ben said a prayer before we took off.

When we arrived in Miami, we all took photos in front of the jet and I posted mine on Instagram, which would come back to haunt me. And although Olivia had classes and was forced to stay behind, her family offered to pick us up at the airport and drop us off at the Loews Hotel in Miami Beach, where everyone but me would spend the weekend.

Yet within four short months, Olivia and I would split up. We were both young, insecure, and on separate paths, and it seemed inevitable as it was happening. But in retrospect, I can't help but sense external forces that seem to have helped us along to our fateful conclusion. Despite her generosity and outward support, Becki seemed to constantly be sowing seeds of doubt. If Olivia had to travel overnight for a medical or school-related conference, Becki would say things like, "What do you suppose she's doing after her meetings?" or "I would never go on a trip without Jerry." She would commiserate with me whenever Olivia had to put in long nights studying or was otherwise caught up in her heavy course load, telling me, "You need a good Christian girl from LU." Enough so that it got into my head, where it festered and finally exploded.

When we broke up, Jerry and Becki just happened to be in Miami. She offered me a shoulder to cry on, and then respite from this unfamiliar pain I was trying to negotiate, and then like clockwork, we were sleeping together again.

While Jerry watched.

CHAPTER 11

TRIAL BY INNUENDO

At a dinner with the Falwell family in March 2014 at
Macchialina—in front of Becki, Trey, Wesley and his wife
Laura, Caroline, the co-owner of the restaurant, and me—Jerry
told us a story about John Gauger, the chief information officer
(CIO) at Liberty and now executive vice president of analyt-
ics, who was like an IT guy for the whole university. Still in his
thirties, he had a side hustle called RedFinch Solutions, which
was described in its LinkedIn profile as "an IT consultancy firm
that specializes in providing timely, cost-effective solutions for
businesses in a variety of industries," and elsewhere as: "This organization primarily operates in the Business Consulting, NEC
["Not Elsewhere Classified"] business/industry within the En-

gineering, Accounting, Research and Management Services sector."

But despite the vagueness of this corporate premise, Red-Finch Solutions operated as an online reputation enhancement firm, the kind of business that can generate hundreds of comments, replies, poll votes, reviews, et cetera, for anything posted online, to the benefit of paying clients. Online reputation management firms also can help drive traffic to positive online posts by placing those posts atop a Google search and knocking everything else down a notch. According to Politico, Jerry had asked Gauger once (not all that successfully, as it turns out) to bury some photos of the family dancing and whooping it up at Wall, a nightclub in the W Hotel in Miami. (Jerry denied the allegations.)

Over dinner, Jerry told us how Gauger had recently been approached by Michael Cohen with an assignment involving Donald Trump. They had met on that campus walkabout in 2012 when Trump spoke at the Convocation, and Cohen reached out to him for advice on how to set up an Instagram account. Turns out CNBC, the leading business network, was sponsoring an online poll of the hundred most influential business figures of the last century. Trump figured he was a shoo-in, but after days of open voting he was still bobbing low in the poll ratings. Cohen's solution was to rig the results. While this was as unprincipled as it was petty, and a ridiculous use of grown men's time and resources, not to mention a dubious enterprise for someone with an extremely lucrative position at a Christian citadel, Gauger, through RedFinch, took on the challenge. The assignment was pretty easy. The trick was how to do it without being discovered.

Gauger's firm successfully manipulated the poll results, pushing Trump up to ninth place mere hours before the voting ended. The next day, CNBC disqualified Trump without providing a reason. Cohen devotes a whole chapter to the episode in his book, titled "How to Rig a Poll." "I knew from past experience that he was a flexible thinker when it came to issues like the one I was confronting on Trump's behalf," Cohen writes of Gauger, begging the question what exactly had they been collaborating on before?

The *Wall Street Journal* later reported that Gauger did the same thing in February 2015 for a Drudge Report poll on possible Republican presidential candidates, where Trump split the pack at number five although he had yet to declare, and then again for Cohen himself, to drive traffic to "a sock-puppet Twitter account" with the aspirational name "@womenforcohen," which repeatedly referred to him as a "pit bull." Gauger was eventually paid out of the same tranche of money earmarked to silence Stormy Daniels (one of the many charges Cohen eventually went to prison for). Gauger was promised an additional $50,000 bonus, which Cohen arbitrarily reduced to between $12,000 and $13,000 and which, according to Gauger, came stuffed in a blue Walmart bag along with a boxing glove once worn by a Brazilian MMA fighter. (Cohen denies these claims.)

In May 2014, I attended Trey's wedding at the Greenbrier, a century-old, five-star luxury resort in White Sulphur Springs, West Virginia. Early on, Becki introduced me to a guy who I believe was her nephew. He was a little older than me, and he wore an implacable smirk the whole time as Becki nattered on about how I was their "business partner from Miami" or "practically family." It stayed with me all weekend. Did everyone know about them and their private kink? No wonder they were so lax about being discovered.

It shouldn't be all that surprising then when Becki whispered to me, "Let's pretend like we're married." I told her to stop being silly. If she was kidding, she kept up the pretense for much of the weekend. Despite my warnings that they needed to be more circumspect in their public behavior, that even their drinking and carousing among friends and family put a target on their backs, it all fell on deaf ears. Their behavior became increasingly brazen and reckless the longer I knew them, making a mockery of the values they held others to, and it gave their enemies a bomb they could set off at any time. As the first and most likely victim of their heedless libertinism, and the one who would get dragged through the tabloids shackled to their golden chariot, I didn't feel good about any of it.

The remainder of the weekend passed without incident, save for Becki and I sneaking away to have sex whenever we could. Then in the first week of August, we all met up for a party on Bobby Moon's wakeboarding boat on the James River in nearby Virginia. Moon was the owner and operator of Construction Management Associates, a company with exclusive contracts with Liberty University worth hundreds of millions of dollars, and which is now "within the scope of" the comprehensive audit being conducted today by accounting firm Baker Tilly of Liberty's finances, according to Liberty. Moon was one of Jerry's best friends, and he launched his company on January 1 of that year with a $750,000 loan from Liberty, just in time to prosper from the university's proposed $1 billion expansion plans. Jerry's ambitions for the campus seemed to have no limits: upgrading sports facilities, building stadiums, a concert hall, a nearby shooting range, and all of it was a superhighway running right through Bobby Moon and his fledgling company. This also proved true of CSE, Inc., another Moon family business that provided construction cranes. The podcast *Gangster Capitalism*, in reviewing a copy of CMA's contract with Liberty, reported that it was guaranteed a minimum of $50 million of business a year, with an additional 2.5 percent fee for CMA, and that their bids were often millions more than that of the competition. Moon also employed Sarah Falwell, Trey's wife, before she was hired by Liberty as executive director of career services in 2019.

It was the middle of the workweek, but everybody worked for Jerry in one way or another, so when the boss says let's party, you close up shop for the day. We spent all afternoon wakeboarding and wakesurfing, then anchored the boat and started blasting music. People who lived along the river started yelling at us—so much so that I thought someone might take a shot at us, but eventually they turned it down and I could breathe a little bit easier. Plenty of people were drunk or tipsy and having a good time, but I stayed relatively sober, as the Falwell kids were there. Then Chris Doyle started grinding on Becki on the dance floor, and vice versa. I had kept my distance from Becki in public out of deference to her family; maybe that's why she was acting out with Chris Doyle. But it could not have been clearer that nobody cared—least of all Jerry.

I transferred to Florida International University for the fall semester of 2014, where I would pursue a bachelor's degree for business administration in finance. With a new job and now a new school, my sometimes unorthodox trajectory seemed to be settling into something resembling a predictable path, and with it my general state of mind. That is until the first week of October, when I received a letter from a local personal injury lawyer asking me to please give him a call. His letter appeared so opaque and harmless that I dialed the number right away.

"Helloooooo, Mr. Granda," boomed the voice from the other end. His manner was exceedingly theatrical and border-line comical. "I have been approached by my clients here"—the Fernandezes—"and as a devout Christian, what they are telling me *breaks my heart*!" He told me that a major scandal was on the verge of breaking due to nefarious actions on my part. As soon as he got that far, I told him, "You'll be hearing from my attorney," and hung up. I called Jerry immediately and told him it sounded like we were being extorted. Jerry said he'd handle it.

Jerry had me call Josh Spector, who was the litigator for Al-ton Hostel, LLC, and he dutifully arranged a meeting with the Fernandezes' lawyer. At that first confab, the lawyer produced several emails that he claimed implied a verbal contract, and that the Fernandezes were entitled to more money. Then he showed Spector naked pictures of Becki. These photos had nothing to do with his client's claim, and he made no effort to tie the two together. The threat, implicitly, was that if we went to trial, cer-tain revelations would emerge in the discovery process or under cross-examination. The lawyer said his clients would settle for $7 million.

When Spector reported back to us and began describing the photos he had seen, my heart sank. It wasn't that salacious pho-tos of Becki had been released into the wild, or that they would almost certainly reveal the embarrassing circumstances of my relationship with the Falwells. It was that every single photo he recounted I was intimately familiar with, since they were all in my possession. If we were searching for a weak link in the chain of title, it looked for all the world like it was me.

There were photos Becki had sent me early in our relation-ship of her topless: sitting on a tractor at their farm, by the barn, and from before I met her, on a family vacation at Banff National Park in Alberta, overlooking Lake Louise. There were photos that had obviously been pulled off social media: Becki and me at Cheeca Lodge (fully dressed), Jerry with a rum and Coke in one hand, and the photo of all of us posed in front of the Liberty jet in Lynchburg, headed back to Miami. There was also a shot of me having ejaculated on Becki's stomach—either at Cheeca or the Gansevoort, I can't be sure—taken with my BlackBerry and with Becki's (and Jerry's) full consent. That photo does not show Becki's face, nor was I in it. But I knew what it was. If there was any sense of relief, it was that there were no naked photos of me.

Spector recommended I get my own attorney to avoid a potential conflict of interest, as he would continue to represent Jerry, Becki, Trey, and me through the LLC, and this had now evolved far beyond a simple business dispute. The photos were obviously stolen, and I had no idea how the Fernandezes had acquired them, but Spector told me, "There's going to be a lot of accusations being thrown around." Since I was new to the world of civil litigation (and didn't really have a budget for legal retainers), Jerry offered to pay for my attorney. With my permission, Spector suggested a friend who he frequently worked with and who had experience with extortion cases: a private attorney in Miami named Aaron Resnick. He had represented a lot of NFL players and other high-dollar athletes (think HBO's *Ballers*). Spector assured me, "This is the guy you want."

I agreed to cooperate with Resnick however he needed me to. I wanted to be 100 percent transparent. I was in possession of all the photos the Fernandezes had, so it made the most sense that they came from me, although I was mystified how that might have happened. It was possible my phone or computer had been hacked, but I didn't know much about how hacking worked. At any rate, I hadn't noticed anything out of the ordinary.

Any normal lawsuit, I'd say let the attorneys handle it and it will play out like it's going to. Not that being sued isn't crazy scary, but I'm prone to obsessing over things, and that's not going to help me in my situation. Except nothing about this so-called lawsuit was normal. In my view, the emails and the verbal contract were merely a pretext. This was a shakedown, pure and simple. The pictures themselves were moot. The fact that the photos might leak, and the embarrassment it would cause us all, was the implicit threat. Powerful people will pay good money to keep their secrets, and the Falwells' particular hobby could not have been more off-brand to the First Family of evangelicalism.

After a meeting with Resnick at his office in downtown Miami, I returned to the parking garage to discover that my 2008 Nissan Ultima wouldn't start. Opening the trunk to get my jumper cables, on the off chance that I could prevail on that legendary generosity Miamians are known for the world over, I made an odd discovery. When Jerry had mock-threatened me (or maybe not so mock) at his farm back in September 2012, the weekend that Trump spoke at the Convocation, I decided to take all the incriminating evidence off my computer—photos, texts, emails—and save it on a flash drive, as insurance in case I ever needed it (or in my darker moments, if something ever happened to me). Since I didn't want to keep it in my apartment, I hid it in a special compartment in the trunk of my car that wasn't obvious unless you knew where to look for it. At some point months before this, I had discovered that the flash drive was missing, although I had no way of knowing how long it had been gone.

But now here it was again, lying out in the open, directly in the center of the trunk space. I have no way to explain this. If someone had broken into my car, maybe the car alarm could have drained the battery. But why would anyone break into a car to return stolen photos? Could it have somehow shaken loose from some other part of the trunk where it had been hiding all this time? But why now, at the exact second the photos were threatening to supernova? And what about all the texts and emails I had stored on the flash drive? If this had been the source of the data leak, why didn't the extortionists include any of those, which would have bolstered their case? Or did the unseen powers that be merely leave this damning artifact here in plain sight to taunt me, to break my spirit, spelling out in implied semaphore, "I know everything!"

I've turned these details over and over in my mind, and I can't make a coherent pattern out of them. Since I had downloaded the photos onto my computer to transfer them onto the flash drive, I kept trying to figure out if someone had hacked my computer, and what digital footprint that would have left on my device. These concepts were far murkier a decade ago, hackers seeming akin to serial killers and criminal masterminds, in the movies at least, capable of anything. This was fairly early in the technology, when the protocols and etiquette of things like camera phones, digital privacy, texting, sexting, and revenge porn were all still another universe away. We understand the permanence of digital files much better now than we did then. Much later, it occurred to me there would be surveillance cameras in the garage and I could check the tape. But this was long past the point where they would have been wiped. I still can't explain what happened with the flash drive.

Tito and his dad threatened to name me in their lawsuit, except there was no lawsuit yet, only the threat of one. Then came mediation. The offers and counteroffers went back and forth indefinitely without ever getting resolved—not until years later when Jerry finally took the initiative. Then in early December, I got a call from Becki while I was walking to class, telling me not to worry about it after all, that "a friend of ours," Michael Cohen, was going to take care of everything—i.e., make the lawsuit "go away." The same Michael Cohen who was Trump's fixer, who I met in Lynchburg nearly two and a half years before—schlubby guy, rumpled suit, quiet. Never misses anything.

Huh.

CHAPTER 12

A FRIEND OF OURS

Between the fall of 2013 (when Olivia and I broke up) and May 2015 (when Angelina and I made it official), Becki and I had sex dozens of times in a variety of locations. In Miami hotel rooms, whenever they could find a pretext to get away. At the Greenbrier the weekend of Trey's wedding. Numerous times at their house in Goode, outside of Lynchburg. And at least once in the private bathroom of Jerry's office at Liberty University. During that last one, Jerry's assistant walked into his office, and he hurriedly intercepted her and walked her back out, inquiring about some pressing issue he made up on the spot.

At the Loews Hotel in South Beach during one of our regular assignations at which Jerry was present (we also frequented the Gale Hotel Miami and the Ritz Carlton in Miami Beach), he pulled out a small handheld camera with a flip screen and began filming us—this time out in the open. At the time, I was still hurting from my recent breakup with Olivia and more numb than anything else, and so I went with it. Afterward, sensing my hesitation, Jerry insisted he'd keep it in the safe in his home office. (Ask Pamela Anderson and Tommy Lee how that worked out.) When I asked them about it later on, they quickly changed the subject. I know of a few other times he filmed us, once each at the other two Miami locations, once in a car, and once at their house. Together with the clandestine tape Becki alluded to early in our relationship, that makes at least six different videos of us having sex floating around somewhere.

No one is supposed to have access to Jerry's private office at the house. Becki treats it as his private respite, and the kids know not to go in there. But Jerry wanted to show me a genealogy of his family once dating back to the 1600s that he was particularly proud of, and while I was in there, I saw a box full of portable hard drives, with some thumb drives and the cube-shaped ones that are usually fire- and waterproof. Why?

In mid-February 2015, under the auspices of their new attorney, the Fernandezes filed a bill of discovery, which is "a pleading that seeks the disclosure of facts known by the adverse party," independent of the recovery of damages. This means that no financial demands will be made until the plaintiff can confidently assess the circumstances of the defendant, as well as the extent of the damage he has caused. In layman's terms, as my attorney explained, it means a fishing expedition, which through the wide-angle lens of the discovery process might turn up so much embarrassing bilge that the defendant has no choice but to settle—hopefully for top dollar. Hence the Fernandezes wanted to depose as many people as possible—Jerry, Becki, Trey, Chris Doyle, me, anyone who had anything to do with the Alton Road investment, I'm sure—and lay claim to any text messages, emails, phone records, photos, and incriminating videos they could find. In lieu of a contract, evidence, pertinent testimony, or a case of any merit, they chose to try and dig up our secrets and sell them back to us at a premium.

Which I guess is how we came to require the services of the illustrious Mr. Cohen. Aside from claiming he was tied to the Russian mob and being kept up nights by future president Trump's nonstop shenanigans, Michael Cohen was also well-connected in Miami. He knew the mayor—he knew everyone. I didn't know much about him—no one did yet in the spring of 2015, I don't think—but I remembered him from Liberty. I was just relieved this was all going to finally get handled. Although he was a licensed attorney, Cohen had graduated from what may be the worst law school in America—Thomas M. Cooley Law School in Lansing, Michigan; Politico ran a headline explicitly proclaiming it as such. It accepts over four-fifths of all applicants, and less than half of all graduates pass the bar on the first try. Not only was Cohen the school's most infamous alumnus, he was class president in 1991. So it's fair to say that whatever Trump saw in him, it was unlikely his legal prowess.

Michael Cohen made his bones in the high-stakes world of New York City taxi medallions, which today you can pick up for a breezy eighty grand apiece, but at their peak in 2014 sold for a million bucks per. He owned thirty-two of them, against which he carried $22 million in debt as of July 2017 (so said the Mueller investigation, which took an interest in him, in its legal filings). I feel confident in suggesting he ran in a colorful crowd and made friends easily. Good thing too, since he began a three-year prison sentence in May 2019 for, among other things, campaign finance violations (i.e., paying hush money to women who claimed sexual dalliances with his erstwhile employer) and lying to Congress about his back-channel machinations to build a Trump Tower in Moscow, plus a host of other improbable violations.

It's hard to know what to make of Michael Cohen. His book *Disloyal*, written mostly in prison, in the law library of the Federal Correctional Institution in Otisville, New York, was released in September 2020, mere months before the election—apparently so as to warn the world that Trump did not plan to leave peacefully, a pretty good tip in retrospect. In it, he spends a fair amount of time on the Falwells. Turns out that he and Becki and Jerry *were* friends of a sort—at least the asymmetrical kind where one friend ingratiates himself by performing impossible favors for the other. They met at New York's Trump Tower in November 2011 as part of an exploratory meeting by candidate Trump, who was then considering a 2012 presidential run, with fifty prominent members of the evangelical community, brokered by preacher Paula White.

As Cohen tells it, "As the two-hour session broke up, another event took place that would come to have a huge impact on the 2016 election, whether God wanted it or not. The genesis of this momentous moment, as you'll see in the pages to come, was my first meeting with Jerry and Becki Falwell and the implications it would have on the future of America. With folks milling around in the hallway of Trump Tower, I fell into a conversation with the couple that would provide the first flutter of a wave to the

butterfly wings flapping that rippled outward and led to the devout and undying devotion to Trump of millions of evangelicals
that still mystifies so many Americans.

"Justin Bieber was the catalyst.

"Go figure."

At that meeting, the Falwells mentioned that they planned
to stay over in Manhattan an extra day, as their daughter Caroline, then twelve, was extremely excited that Justin Bieber was in
town to perform on the *Today Show*, set up outside on Rocke-
feller Plaza. Cohen was able to pull some strings and get the
whole family VIP passes, including a backstage meeting with the
pop idol (so he implies). He also takes this moment in his story
to spool out what amounts to a pro tip: "Part of the art to being
a fixer, doing small and big things for people, was never, ever
asking for anything in return—for myself, that is. For others, I
was more than happy to call in a chit or IOU or however you
want to describe the sense of obligation . . . This particular favor
and another of greater significance would come due in 2016,
to the enormous benefit not of me, but the political prospects
of candidate Donald Trump." His account is accompanied by
a full-page photo of the three of them. (He describes Becki as
"beautiful and vivacious, with a ton of energy and life.")

That second favor is also addressed in the book, although
he hopelessly mangles the details, down to whose lawyer he was
threatening over the phone. In what he terms "a catch and kill
operation," Cohen relates the story of how the Falwells met me
and our lives came to be terminally intertwined.

"They'd stayed at the five-star Fontainebleau Hotel and soak-
ing up the sun the pair had become friendly with a kid working
at the pool. Jerry called him a pool boy." He said they'd stayed in

touch with the pool boy and there was a business "deal that was never consummated," there were hard feelings, "the kid had filed a lawsuit," and the pool boy now had "embarrassing" photos of his wife (he describes the one of Becki on the tractor), although not "pornographic, or anything like that." Most egregiously, "[T]he pool boy was now threatening to shop the photographs to publications as a way to pressure the Falwells to settle the lawsuit on favorable terms." In quick succession, Cohen puts the Falwells at ease, assures them this is personal for him as well, describes the two of them as "like family" and, mustering that legal acumen they teach you at Thomas M. Cooley Law School in Lansing, Michigan, tells them, "I won't call the pool boy, I'll talk to his lawyer."

Then for another full page of breathless prose, he recounts how he got my lawyer on the phone, "asked if he was still representing the pool boy," and reproduced actual conversations where "the pool boy had menaced the Falwells." That makes seven times he uses the term "pool boy" in ten paragraphs. The he goes for the jugular—accusing the lawyer's client (me) of extortion, demanding I return all the photos, plus the names of anyone who has seen them, by 3:00 p.m., or he'll see that the Falwells file a complaint with the FBI. This the lawyer does, quaking in his semi-brogue oxfords, and the matter is effortlessly resolved. "There it was: my second chit with the Falwells," Cohen concludes. "In good time, I would call in this favor, not for me, but for the Boss, at a crucial moment on his journey to the Presidency."

Okay, maybe it's not so simple to fact-check niggling details from inside prison, including a medium-security Club Fed like the one where he was doing time. But even by that low bar, Cohen's version fails miserably—amounting to little more than self-serving mythology. Our business deal was not "never consummated" since there are legal filings for the LLC, easily accessible to lawyers or the public, with me as an equity partner. I hadn't filed any lawsuit—I was a target of the lawsuit, and in fact continued to participate in the Falwells' public ruse for most of the next half decade, including after the story broke. The tractor photo was the least of their worries, as it was the most easily explained; at least one of the photos was explicitly pornographic, and I didn't threaten to shop them around to pressure Jerry into settling a lawsuit I hadn't filed because then I would be guilty of extortion.

As for the lawyer he allegedly talked to (who reputedly claimed to represent me as a client), Cohen must have had that conversation with one of the Fernandezes' attorneys, because the bill of discovery quietly languished and disappeared.

We hoped for good.

CHAPTER 13

INTO THE WOODS

As far as I knew at the time, Michael Cohen was the right guy in the right place at the right time. But as soon as he came into the picture, weird things began happening in my world.

In 2015, I lived at my parents' house in Miami. Too many times to count, I would discover my car door unlocked, although I knew I had locked it. Random items would go missing—a book bag at school; the tuxedo I was going to wear to my cousin's wedding. Vans were constantly parked outside my house, so often that it became a standing joke in my family. I would spot what I assumed were private investigators following me in traffic or parked outside my parents' house at night. One particular couple, a man and a woman, I noticed watching me, and then later the same day I recognized them again in a different vehicle. I saw the same couple outside my apartment in 2019, after I had relocated to Washington, DC. The last time, they were being so obvious it's as if they wanted me to notice them. None of this was doing any favors for my state of mind.

Jerry and Becki met me for dinner at the Loews Hotel in Miami Beach in April 2015, and Jerry said he planned to endorse Donald Trump for the Republican presidential nomination. This came as a surprise, since Trump himself hadn't formally announced his candidacy yet (that would happen in June), and because Ted Cruz was widely thought to have the inside track on the evangelical vote. Cruz would be in for a rude awakening, I thought.

After dinner, Becki and I went back to their cabana—no sex, just to talk privately. I confessed that I had a new girlfriend, Angelina, someone I had met at school and had been going out with since March, and that I wanted to make it exclusive. That meant I needed to break it off again. I told her I felt depressed and jaded. My relationship with her and Jerry had damaged my perception of relationships in general. Angelina was a chance for a fresh start. If she truly felt like she said she did, she would allow me this chance to be happy. She began to cry and tried to lay another one of her guilt trips on me, but I had prepared myself for it, and I didn't budge. I finally compromised by agreeing to continue our emotional connection like I did when I started dating Olivia.

When I left their cabana, Jerry was sitting by the pool, and I joined him. He offered to buy out my equity stake in the Alton Road property for $1.1 million. In addition, he offered me an equity stake in the La Quinta Hotel in Lynchburg, which would be the equivalent of $50,000 per year. He went through all the terms, and I didn't interrupt him. When he was finished, I accepted his offer, but he advised me that he thought the lawsuit with the Fernandezes would come back around eventually. Michael Cohen aside (although I would assign more credit to our legal team), it would never be over until we had a settlement. The threat of a lawsuit was the same as a lawsuit. So this sudden windfall would have to wait until the matter was resolved, which meant until the Fernandezes made their move. I felt like Jerry and I were both being extorted—him for the photos and me for half of my equity share, since I couldn't sell my stake without risking half the sale price if the Fernandezes prevailed in court. In essence, their pending legal claim (actual or implicit) handcuffed me to the property.

I reminded Jerry I had been nothing but compliant thus far, and that I was loyal to my friends and partners. When Tito and his dad first started gumming up the works, I'm the one who counseled Jerry they were looking to play us off against one another, and suggested we raise our profile on social media, posting lots of pictures of us all together, as a way to needle them. One series we posted that particularly irritated them was of Jerry, Becki, and me at a Miami Dolphins game with the Huizenga family—owners of the Miami Dolphins, Florida Marlins, and Florida Panthers—in their private box. The Fernandezes' attorney responded by complaining that we weren't taking their demands seriously.

I knew that Jerry had fielded offers from other investors in the $5 to $7 million range, and I was aware that lawsuits can drag on for years. I wanted out now so I could invest on my own and enjoy my life with Angelina, without Becki pestering me.

I told him this had all been an interesting diversion in my life, but that I needed to get back on the main highway. Whatever he needed me to do to resolve the issue with the Fernandezes, whenever it came to a head, I'd be there for him. But I wanted out now.

This triggered an unflattering side of Jerry. When you hear him speak in public or see him on TV, he's ill at ease in front of a crowd, stumbling through his words. In social situations he's usually buzzed and pretty affable. But there's another side that the people around him see but the public doesn't: He can be a screamer, verbally abusive to the people he works with and ruthless about getting his way. I've seen him bully Becki and reduce her to tears. He yelled at her in front of my mother once. He was on her about her weight, and she was constantly trying to maintain her petite figure. A few times when I encouraged her to finish her meal, Jerry would make pig noises. He thought he was being funny, but trust me, he wasn't.

This time he leaned in and lowered his voice so that no one could hear. He reminded me that they still had explicit sex videos of Becki and me. He threatened to send them to Angelina with Becki's face blurred out. He also insisted I had to continue the emotional connection with Becki—the daily text messages, nightly phone calls, all of it. It came with a flash of anger I had rarely seen, but learned to be wary of.

In hindsight, I should have told him to go stuff himself and filed a police report, but the truth is that I wanted an amicable split from the business partnership. Plus I was young, and I still had a problem saying no and establishing boundaries. So I didn't, and now here we are.

Jerry's biggest miscalculation in this whole thing was not

trusting me 100 percent. I assured him that I never would have conspired with Tito, I would never commit a felony, and if I did, I certainly wouldn't do it with a hothead like Tito. The guy couldn't walk into a bar without getting his ticket punched. Plus it would have been idiotic for me to hand over the photos to them. The Fernandezes' boneheaded shakedown and threatened lawsuit was what was keeping us from selling the property and pocketing a healthy profit. Just as it was Jerry's refusal to go to the FBI in the first place that gave them a clear lane to move forward. They should have been clear-cut like timber, and we all should have taken a step back and watched them topple.

In the fall semester of 2015, something happened that changed the game for me. The number of incidents of me being watched or followed had risen substantially. The tipping point came one day after a business class at FIU, when I stopped to get something to eat. As I ate in my car in a Taco Bell parking lot listening to a podcast, I heard a tap on my window. I looked up to see a white guy standing there, maybe in his forties, wearing a black hoodie and balaclava mask that covered most of his face. He was holding a handgun. It wasn't pointed at me, but he held it so that I could clearly see it. I froze and time stopped. I have never experienced pure, crystalline fear like I did in that moment.

He signaled for me to roll down the window. I fumbled for the switch and when the glass lowered, he said, "Keep your mouth shut." Then he turned and walked away, disappearing around a corner. I didn't follow him, and I didn't snap a picture of him with my phone. I didn't even respond to what he said. I just drove home in a haze. I tried to think who could have been behind this, but the problem was that every character in the story seemed like a prime candidate. There was no way to narrow it down. I still have no idea who threatened me—or why. Later that evening, Angelina could see I was clearly spooked and asked me what happened. I said, "I can't tell you. But this is getting crazy."

I didn't report this incident to the police. Maybe it's because I'm half Mexican and all my mother's stories of growing up in Mexico City reflected how corrupt the local police are. In her world, you never called the police, unless maybe if someone got murdered. They're not going to do anything unless you bribe them, and then they're just as likely to take a bigger bribe from the other side and make your life hell. An extended family member on my mother's side, a real estate investor in Mexico City who is quite wealthy, was the victim of an express kidnapping—his daughter was driving their Mercedes when a van pulled up beside her and men with assault rifles entered her car. He had to negotiate a settlement with them to get her back, and the police were useless from start to finish. That's because in Mexico, the police work for the criminals. You hear these kinds of stories your whole life and it rubs off on you.

So it never occurred to me to report what I considered a very credible death threat to the authorities. Instead, I began to constantly look over my shoulder, and always checked the back seat to make sure no one was hiding there. To this day, I'm often filled with anxiety, and suffer from panic attacks.

That October, Wesley Falwell and his girlfriend Laura got married at the Albemarle Estate, part of the Trump Winery in Virginia, about ninety minutes northeast of the Falwells' farm. As a member of their "extended family," I attended, with Angelina as my plus-one. It was the Falwells' first time meeting her, and I wanted them to see that we were happy, and to sever any lingering romantic ties Becki might still harbor. The reception was restricted to family and close friends, most of whom were Liberty students, which Laura had graduated from and now worked at. Bottles of Casamigos tequila adorned all the tables. Jerry was drunk and took to the dance floor to grind up on students, which I'm pretty sure is prohibited by the Liberty Code.

During the party, I saw Jerry sitting on the couch with a student, his arm draped around her while he whispered in her ear. She looked noticeably uncomfortable, slowly trying to push him away. Jerry would later send me a photo of the same woman in the kitchen at the farm lifting her dress up to reveal her panties. He claimed he was making fun of her "granny panties," that it was all good clean fun, but I can't imagine she granted him permission to send it to me and God knows how many others. And I've personally witnessed him grope female students who came up to him during a walking tour of the Liberty campus. Not flagrantly, maybe, but to where it seemed inappropriate. It was usually met with a shrug and a response of "that's just Jerry being Jerry." Whatever unconfirmed suspicions there were, they could always be folded into this avuncular image of him as an incorrigible flirt and rascal.

It's all right there in living color if you look for it: dancing with abandon, drinking to excess, nightclubbing, sexual libertinism, a corporate jet at their personal disposal, illicit adventures, and endless amounts of money they effectively siphoned off a committed and faithful student body—all of it common knowledge among their inner circle. It's *The Handmaid's Tale*, where a ruling elite in the state of Gilead, a theocracy that has displaced most of the continental US, enjoys a lavish lifestyle, indulges in every taboo and flouts the laws and moral strictures that bind everyone else, their evangelical true believers, all in the name of privilege.

On December 4, 2015, two days after a pair of violent extremists attacked their coworkers' Christmas party in San Bernardino, California, killing fourteen and seriously wounding twenty-two, Jerry declared at the regular Friday Convocation, "It just blows my mind that the President of the United States [Barack Obama][says] that the answer to circumstances like that is more gun control. If some of those people in that community center had what I have in my back pocket right now. . . ." He was interrupted at this point by applause and some cheering. "Is it illegal to pull it out? I don't know . . . I've always thought that if more good people had concealed-carry permits, then we could end those Muslims before they walked in . . . and killed them." The last three words were drowned out by an ovation. "Let's teach them a lesson if they ever show up here."

Reading it online in Miami, I thought he was playing to the cheap seats, but I also noted that these were favorite talking points of his friend Donald Trump. Angelina, a second-generation immigrant, was livid, and questioned why I was still friends with these people. I tried to tell her, "You don't know them; you have no idea what they're capable of." I basically felt like I had no option. And in fact, I did challenge Jerry in a text exchange, and he agreed he could have been more careful in his word choice, before changing the subject to compliment me on how the hostel was running smoothly. His comments proved wildly controversial, and he appeared in the *Washington Post* and elsewhere defending them and deflecting the criticism. Maybe that was his goal all along.

As Jerry told me he would, he publicly endorsed Trump on January 18, 2016, during a Liberty Convocation, with Trump once again in attendance. This was at the start of the primary season and only days ahead of the Iowa caucus, famously a bellwether for the most promising candidates, at a time when Ted Cruz and Mike Huckabee believed they had the evangelical vote sewn up between them.

Jerry's endorsement had wide repercussions, as he singlehandedly made it acceptable for religious conservatives to vote for Trump, despite the pussy grabbing, casual racism, public bullying, and palpable sense of grievance that were to become his signature traits. If the heir to the great Falwell dynasty said it was okay, then who was the humble layman to challenge his reasoning?

So was Michael Cohen responsible for brokering Jerry's endorsement for Donald Trump, a key factor in securing him the presidency? Certainly Cohen does everything in his book to take credit for it, shy of claiming an outright quid pro quo, albeit in mangled syntax: "this momentous moment," "the first flutter of a wave to the butterfly wings flapping that rippled outward . . ." It's clear that what he's getting at is that we live in a different world now, and for better or worse, we have Michael Cohen to thank for it. Jerry is adamant there was no quid pro quo. Cohen merely says he brought the Falwells to the table. Quid pro quo implies blackmail, extortion—crimes of opportunity, where someone agrees to do something against their will. People assume the Falwells panicked and were grateful for Cohen's intervention, willing to do anything in exchange for making their problem go away. That may be true, but it doesn't overshadow the fact that they longed to be a part of Trump's universe. After

Cohen got involved, the Falwells' behavior became more brazen, and their speech more intemperate. They traveled in higher circles with greater access, like showing up backstage at an Elton John concert. Jerry even became friends (of a sort) with Trump acolyte Kanye West. Their influence broadened, with Becki named to the advisory board of Women for Trump.

With Trump as president, and with the implicit protection, full force, and authority of the United States government, they would become untouchable. It was the sort of power the whole family had been secretly dreaming about for generations. Similarly, if you're Michael Cohen, rather than threaten them, shake them down, or further exacerbate their fears, the far more subtle play would be to convince the Falwells that with Trump in power, they would all be welcome within his sphere of influence. Power like that would take care of past photos and future photos alike.

CHAPTER 14

STRANGE BEDFELLOWS

In March 2016, Angelina and I took a vacation to Mexico, where we stayed in an apartment that my parents owned in the heart of Mexico City. One day into our trip, we came home to find the apartment had been ransacked. I checked under the sofa, where I'd hidden my laptop, and it was gone. The perpetrators took paintings off the wall and stacked them on the floor, and smashed up random furniture. The laptop was the only thing missing, although there was jewelry and an expensive watch lying on the bed in plain view. Luckily, the laptop was brand new so there was nothing of consequence on it, plus it was a PC and password protected, and I was able to wipe it remotely. But it's worth noting that there was no history of burglaries in the building. Needless to say, we were both seriously rattled by this intrusion, which seemed suspiciously of a piece with all the other inexplicable things that had entered my life. After checking every room and closet, not knowing whether an intruder would lunge out at us, we immediately upgraded to a hotel with armed security.

I've spoken with sources since then who said it sounds like the handiwork of one of the private security agencies that combine intelligence tactics with psyops, where the psychological dislocation is a big part of it. All I know is that once Jerry hitched his wagon to Trump, all of these people started showing up in my world: publicist Matt Hiltzik, whose client roster included Harvey Weinstein, Jared Kushner, and Ivanka Trump, and whose protégé Hope Hicks became the White House communications director and later an adviser to the president; litigator Michael Bowe, who represented both Jerry against the university and Trump against an FBI investigation into collusion with the Kremlin; and Charlie Kirk, cofounder with Jerry of the Falkirk Center, a multimillion-dollar think tank on the Liberty Campus with a hard-line conservative pedigree and agenda. I believe that Jerry saw this as his destiny, and a path forward from the moral strictures of his father's faith. Consequently, I believe Trump and those looking out for his interests were aware of my interactions with Jerry, through Michael Cohen and possibly others, and sought to exert damage control where necessary.

After the Mexico City incident, which I was keeping close to the vest, I had my lawyer, Aaron Resnick, tell Jerry's attorneys that I really wanted out of the deal, regardless of what they were threatening. Whoever was behind this, if they were willing to follow me to another country now just to intimidate me, while targeting my girlfriend in the balance, then that seemed to me like things were escalating. I felt I was increasingly in danger, and I wanted to sever my ties with the Falwell family and this entire world that I didn't belong in and wanted no part of. A few days before he was to speak at the Republican National Convention in July 2016, Jerry texted me with some good news. I still have the text thread:

Jerry: Trey says there is enough for you and he to net $600,000 each after taxes. The LOI [Letter of Intent] is non-binding and we can back out anytime. Susan [Gale, the real estate agent for the seller] is pushing hard for us to sign because she is leaving town tomorrow. I recommend we sign, then spend the next couple weeks crunching the numbers to make sure we are right.

Jerry: What do you think?

Me: In class. I'll text you in a few min when we go on break.

Me: If you're sure that we can net at least $600,000 after all expenses and personal taxes then yes let's sign it.

Jerry: Okay we'll back out if we can't. Thanks Gian

Me: OK sounds good

Me: When are we going to sign this?

Jerry: Now but we have 30 days to back out

Me: Ok sounds good

Jerry: Keep your fingers crossed and keep confidential

Jerry: Please

But again, nothing ever seemed to happen with it.

As the election approached, Jerry's natural instinct for caution took a back seat to the exuberance of the moment. All those groups that had galvanized at the dawn of the Reagan era were now a voting bloc and power base, and this was their moment. And right there in the wings, waiting for his moment in the media spotlight, was Jerry Falwell Jr., a newly crowned kingmaker to rival his father.

On November 1, one week before the election, Jerry sent out a statement of support for Donald Trump, something that no president of the university had ever done, and an action that recklessly jeopardized their nonprofit status, without which their business model would be rendered worthless. Nonprofit was the gate holding back the stampede of taxes; if they were forced to compete on a level playing field, it would expose the lie at the heart of their enterprise.

"Before this critical election, I feel compelled to share a personal experience with Hillary Clinton," it began. "The year was 1989. I was serving as general counsel for Liberty University just two years after graduating from the University of Virginia

School of Law." The university then in dire financial straits, Jerry's job was to keep the wolf from the door. His search for much-needed capital led him to a Little Rock investor, Stephens, Inc.

> The attorneys for Stephens, Inc., were a small firm in Little Rock that seemed competent but at the same time were extremely arrogant, condescending, and disrespectful to all of us. They had an attitude of superiority like we had never experienced before. They soon began to push Liberty hard to abandon its Christian traditions and doctrinal foundations. Their argument was that Liberty could save a few dollars by issuing tax exempt bonds instead of taxable bonds. At the time, Virginia law did not permit pervasively sectarian universities from issuing tax exempt bonds. Liberty refused to make any changes that were core to our mission and the Virginia Supreme Court ruled that Liberty could not issue the cheaper tax exempt bonds because of our Christian mission.

Something about that experience persistently nagged at me, but I couldn't put my finger on it. Not long ago, I was looking through the old files and was shocked to realize that the bond counsel that had attempted to force Liberty to abandon its Christian mission years earlier was none other than the Rose Law Firm! By then, Bill Clinton was president and the Rose Law Firm had become famous from the many Clinton scandals in the 1990s. He dutifully ticks off the well-worn names of the law partners on the masthead—Hillary Rodham Clinton, Webb Hubbell (centerpiece of the infamous Whitewater land deal),

Vince Foster ("who was mysteriously found dead in a park a few years later")—successfully dredging up two decades of right-wing conspiracy theories and institutional grievance. "I have no doubt that, if elected, one of Hillary Clinton's prime targets will be the religious freedoms of all people of faith across our nation. The federal government is already using Title IX to attack the religious freedoms of faith-based colleges and universities."

And then, for good measure, this tag:

"The national media, which I consider a wing of the Clinton campaign, recently pushed the false story that a significant number of Liberty University students were opposing Donald Trump." The story, he insinuates, was based on a specious petition signed by outliers and provocateurs. "But facts are often inconvenient. A poll taken yesterday of a random sample of 1,500 Liberty residential students revealed that 78% are voting for Trump, 4% for Hillary, and 18% for other candidates or who declined to answer."

But there was mounting opposition to this sudden militancy in Liberty's implied mission. Jerry took great pains to frame it as one man's opinion, a regular Joe the Chancellor with some things to get off his chest, but not everyone was buying it. Many of his critics opposed the endorsement itself—any endorsement—which went against Liberty's stated mission and represented an existential threat to the university. Meanwhile, they were selling Trump promotional gear on campus, and many in Trump's orbit regularly cycled through the Convocation.

One such critic, Mark DeMoss, chairman of the executive committee of the Liberty board, came from a prominent family of conservative political donors. His father, Arthur DeMoss, was a former New York bookie turned insurance magnate who literally had a tent-show revival conversion and embraced evangelical Christianity, pledging his fortune to advance its agenda (while locking in a loyal clientele whose clean living made them good actuarial risks). He ultimately contributed $20 million to build DeMoss Hall, one of the largest buildings on the Liberty campus. Meanwhile, the Arthur S. DeMoss Foundation spearheaded campaigns against abortion and gay rights, cultivating a worldview that *Time* magazine called "a vision of a Christian America some find overzealous." Mark's sister Deborah worked as an aide to North Carolina senator Jesse Helms, chairman of the Foreign Relations Committee, where her sympathies for Reagan-era monkey business in Central America in the eighties earned her the sobriquet "Death Squad Debbie."

Mark DeMoss, by comparison, was a business Republican in the Mitt Romney mold. A former Liberty graduate and one-time chief of staff for Falwell Sr., for thirty years DeMoss ran an Atlanta-based public relations firm that catered to a host of evangelical and faith-based clients, including the Billy Graham ministry, the Southern Baptist Convention, and commercial clients such as Hobby Lobby and Chick-fil-A. There has always been a faction of the Liberty community loyal to Jerry, and one of equal stature that leans to his brother, Jonathan, and Thomas Road Baptist Church. DeMoss clearly favored the latter.

In broad terms, Jonathan is more low-key than his older brother—both less convivial and less irascible. Jerry is outwardly casual, approachable, fun, while Jonathan is the more pious of the two, and possibly a more likely heir to his father's ministry and legacy. If Jerry Sr. famously brought religion into politics, then Jonathan represents the former and Jerry the latter. There is an unresolved tension between the two camps, as well as the brothers themselves, that has emerged since the death of the family patriarch.

But after Jerry went all in on Trump, DeMoss did what none of Jerry's critics had done before: he took his grievances to the *Washington Post*, echoing what many were saying about Trump privately, inside and outside of organized religion: "The bullying tactics of personal insult have no defense—and certainly not for anyone who claims to be a follower of Christ. That's what's disturbing to so many people." Although they had reportedly discussed the matter privately, Jerry seemed sandbagged by the interview, calling DeMoss's comments "puzzling." The two appeared to agree to disagree, as DeMoss suggested in the article.

Seven weeks later, however, at the next meeting of the board's executive committee, DeMoss was relieved of his chairmanship. He resigned from the full board not long after. Several other high-profile campus figures—including several mega-donors, executive vice president Neal Askew, and Ron Godwin, a close friend and confidant of Falwell Sr. (and the last one to see him alive)—followed DeMoss out the door.

In a final fusillade of petulance, Jerry had DeMoss Hall renamed "Arthur S. DeMoss Hall," effectively obliterating the memory of the son by celebrating the memory of the father. If anyone would understand this type of insult, it would be Jerry Falwell Jr.

CHAPTER 15

CRISIS MANAGEMENT

Another one of these Trump characters I found suddenly spinning in our orbit was the Manhattan publicist and crisis management expert Matthew Hiltzik. He showed up, as I remember it, around the same time as Michael Cohen, but he insists he doesn't know Cohen. Of course, Matt Hiltzik only speaks to the press off the record, and only then to establish under what conditions he will speak at all, and in the service of keeping what he doesn't want said out of print. And whatever I did hear him say, I'm not allowed to tell you. So if there's any connection between Michael Cohen and Matthew Hiltzik, I can't find it.

What I do know is that at some point, probably early 2015, Jerry hired Hiltzik, who for many years, helped preserve Harvey

Weinstein's cuddly public persona before his epic fall from grace, having served as the head of corporate communications for Weinstein's Miramax Films from 1999 to 2005. More recently, in 2017, as Weinstein was slowly circling the drain, Hiltzik was one of many who cycled through the Miramax offices to offer advice, according to *Vanity Fair*. Soon after, he reportedly met with writer Ronan Farrow, then working on one of the stories that would seal Weinstein's fate. As actress Rose McGowan alleged in her 2019 legal complaint against Weinstein, his lawyers, and Black Cube, which was ultimately dismissed, "In or around April 2017, Farrow received calls and texts from publicist Matthew Hiltzik, who reached out to Farrow on Weinstein's behalf. Hiltzik told Farrow that Weinstein could clear up any allegations that McGowan might be making. When Farrow said that he could not talk about his investigation, Hiltzik told Farrow that Weinstein was agitated and upset. According to Hiltzik, Weinstein said other news outlets had investigated Weinstein but determined allegations about Weinstein to be unfounded. Hiltzik warned Farrow that Weinstein would not be taking action immediately, but that he was going to do something. Hiltzik advised Farrow to put his investigation on the back burner." (This follows beat for beat an account by Farrow in his 2019 book *Catch and Kill.*)

Hiltzik is one of the world's most successful crisis management specialists. There's a good chance that anyone on his client roster is having the worst day of their life. He represents himself as the good guy in almost any situation—a decent fellow, making the best of a bad world—as one might expect from someone whose business is traipsing through minefields of the public follies of private monsters. And Hiltzik has a perfectly reasonable explanation for these and probably any other allegations ever made against him. I know this because my cowriter, Mark Ebner, spent an hour and ten minutes on the phone asking him these and other questions, all of which he had answers for, albeit off the record.

Before going to work for Miramax, Hiltzik got his law degree at Fordham. He says on his company website (Hiltzik Strategies) that he is "an active member of the New York State Bar Association," which would seem to imply that if it ever comes down to it, he can claim attorney-client privilege. After law school, Hiltzik served as press secretary and executive director of the New York State Democratic Committee, where he worked on campaigns for Chuck Schumer, Eliot Spitzer, and, in 2000, Hillary Clinton in her successful run for the US Senate. His work with these major players in the Democratic Party allows him to maintain—as he often does—that he is being ecumenical and broad-minded in representing politicians of a partisan bent other than his own

Case in point is Donald J. Trump. Hiltzik has said he considers Ivanka Trump a friend and has long handled her product line, and he did work for Jared Kushner's Manhattan real estate company for a number of years. He was hired by American Media, Inc., publisher of the *National Enquirer*, for one month after the election to field media inquiries for Karen McDougal about her purported ten-month affair with Donald Trump, for which AMI paid $150,000 for the rights to her story. The McDougal story never ran, and the *Enquirer*'s $150,000 was reimbursed by Trump, which was another of the many things that sent Michael Cohen to prison. McDougal later filed suit claiming she was duped into signing a contract giving AMI exclusive rights, hence the ability to keep her from commenting on it until after the election, all of which, McDougal alleged, was done in collusion with the Trump campaign. This is the literal meaning of the phrase "catch and kill," the title of Ronan Farrow's book on his reporting of both the McDougal and Weinstein stories, among others, and the term is widely associated with the *Enquirer* in particular. For his part, according to Talking Points Memo, Hiltzik claimed he provided counsel to neither McDougal nor AMI, then or later, and declined further comment.

Hiltzik was also a mentor to White House director of strategic communications and later Trump adviser Hope Hicks, as he was to Josh Raffel, who *Newsweek* called "Jared Kushner's right-hand man."

The first time I heard of Hiltzik was when he had at least one conference call with Jerry and Becki in 2015 about how to counter the Fernandezes' shakedown. Later, in 2017, his company prepared talking points for Jerry's appearance on the Fox News Channel's *Fox & Friends* to promote the Digital Wellness Center, a rebranded version of Gaming Detox that Jerry was trying to push forward as a program at Liberty. (This was roughly the same time frame as when Hiltzik was allegedly cornering Ronan Farrow in a dark alley.) It was to be part of Liberty's Center for Academic Support and Advising Services—now located in Arthur S. DeMoss Hall—which was all great, except that they never bothered to license the idea from me or made any financial arrangements for its appropriation. When the segment ran on Fox in April 2017, Jerry referred to me as "a friend of ours [who] had a video game addiction," or words to that effect. I congratulated him on the story but added it was disappointing I wasn't even named. I had become a footnote in my own story.

In May 2017, Angelina and I moved in together. We met Jerry and Becki for dinner one night in Miami. As with Olivia before her, Angelina had no idea of my true relationship with the Falwells. As far as she knew, I was like an adopted son to them, and we owned a commercial property together. That night, we finally told them about the stolen laptop in Mexico City from a year before, and there was an awkward silence afterward. I described how weird things had started happening as soon as Michael Cohen and Matt Hiltzik had entered the picture. Jerry denied any involvement and assured me that if anyone had greenlit anything of the kind, that it was done without his knowledge or authorization, but I didn't necessarily believe him.

Two nights later, I had dinner with Jerry and Becki alone. Jerry bragged how Trump senior adviser Steve Bannon had called and offered him a task force position, but he had declined. While he didn't explain why, later in a *Vanity Fair* feature on the Falwells, Jerry mentioned that Trump, Bannon, and Ivanka lobbied him to serve as secretary of education, which he turned down because of the sizable pay cut. There may have also been the daunting process of being vetted by the administration and Congress, but who knows? I had noticed a new arrogance about him ever since he fell into Trump's orbit. And it wasn't merely his demeanor either. He looked more assertive and authoritative. His new status drove him to appear more statesmanlike, the same image his father had cultivated but failed to achieve, as his statements grew less prudent and public sentiment turned against him. I credit Hiltzik with that as well. I asked Jerry if he had ever considered running for office, and he said it was better to be a kingmaker than the king.

The following month, we refinanced the mortgage and all three partners took out a tax-free equity distribution of $100,000 apiece from the LLC. This served to momentarily ease tensions over the buyout, and the protracted negotiations that were like a constant grind in the background. I also initiated a joint venture project proposal with Russell Galbut, the major South Beach developer with properties immediately adjacent to us on Alton Road. He had approached us in 2015 looking to buy us out, but I suggested that Jerry wait because I thought he was lowballing us. Two years later, I cold-called him to propose a joint development project that would combine our two adjacent undeveloped lots into a single eco-friendly luxury residential mid-rise building. He was intrigued enough to want to follow up, and I put him in touch with Jerry and Trey. Shortly after that phone call we hired an architect to draft a feasibility analysis. Based on the proposal we developed with Marcus & Millichap, a commercial real estate brokerage firm, the project would have comprised 57,000 square feet, six stories, ninety residential units, a surfaced garage and street-level retail. It would have cost roughly $11 million, and based on a projected net operating income of $1.5 million a year, would today be worth between $20 and $25 million.

Jerry invited Galbut aboard the 165-foot yacht owned by billionaire Liberty donor Rick Hendrick, owner of Hendrick Motorsports (the university sponsors its own NASCAR driver, former Liberty student William Byron, as part of Hendrick's NASCAR team) and a NASCAR Hall of Famer, down in the Florida Keys. Galbut also made it clear he would be interested in visiting Liberty and meeting Donald Trump. And although the project never got built, Jerry texted me after he first spoke to Galbut, saying, "You really impressed me today. One of the best signs of a good businessman is being willing to change all plans, no matter how emotionally invested you are in them."

On August 25, 2017, an article on our hostel appeared in Politico. Writer Brandon Ambrosino, an openly gay Liberty graduate (class of 2011), got a tip that Jerry Falwells II and III were among the owners of a high-volume South Beach youth hostel located in "perhaps the gayest 6 square miles in the United States" and decided to have some fun with it. Headlined "My Weekend at the Falwells' South Beach Flophouse," with the hyperbolic subhead, "Liberty University presents itself as a temple of virtue. But its founding family's secret Miami hostel is a cesspool of vice," he delivers a first-person travelogue as he and his partner Andy contend with this "dilapidated boarding house" in a "rundown stretch of South Beach," its "stench of general decay and cigarette smoke . . . overpowering." He contrasts Liberty's buttoned-down moral code, especially toward all things "gay-friendly," with the stop-motion ironies that saturate this squalid landscape: a notice posted out front advising NO SOLICITING, FUNDRAISING, POLITICS, SALESMEN, RELIGION prompts the observation that Liberty president Jerry Falwell Jr. "pretty much embodies everything on that sign." The rolling hedonism of the beach-adjacent crowds reminds him that at Liberty, "all manner of vice is prohibited," a zero-tolerance policy that would hardly tolerate the drinking, smoking, strip-club flyers, "free shuttles to local bars," marijuana masked by incense, louche sleeping arrangements, and on-site liquor store rarely outside your field of vision. He understandably finds particularly rankling this direct quote from the Liberty Way: ". . . [H]omosexual conduct or the encouragement or advocacy of any form of sexual behavior that would undermine the Christian identity or faith mission of the University" is expressly forbidden.

Following up on an article he had written the previous October on Falwell's controversial Trump endorsement, for which he had interviewed Jerry, with Trey sitting in, Ambrosino identified the source of tension at Liberty as less about politics and more the "frustration over real or perceived double standards." Faculty members there are under a gag rule, which the administration defends as protecting their tax-exempt status by precluding political endorsements—a position hard to countenance with Jerry's recent oversharing. A brief rundown of the Alton Hostel, LLC, names me (the first publication to do so), and cites a Facebook post documenting a dinner at Macchialina. He also flags a house that Liberty sold to Trey, allegedly at fair-market value, and summarizes the cautionary tale of Mark DeMoss. And then, tying it all together, a presciently uncharitable view of Liberty's financial strategy: "With this in mind, it's not a stretch to view Liberty's online business model—which saved the school from ruin and brings in most of its profit—as something of a slumlord scenario: Keep costs low, bring in struggling customers looking for a bargain, and give them a low-quality product. Not unlike the Falwells' Miami hostel."

At Hiltzik's encouragement, Jerry wrote a response in a statement issued by the university: "The fact is that Trey and his business partner, Giancarlo Granda, identified a distressed property in Miami Beach, which they purchased with bank financing at a very opportune time in a location that has seen significant new developments as a result of extensive infrastructure upgrades and investments by the City of Miami Beach including a new hospital across the street. The property was recently independently appraised by the bank that financed the property, and the value has increased by almost 40 percent in just 4½ years."

I had the queasy feeling we had dodged a bullet, though I worried the article and Jerry's response was only going to invite more scrutiny.

On August 31, the Fernandezes finally filed suit in Miami against Jerry, me, Trey, Becki, the Alton Hostel, LLC, and Comeback Inn, LLC, for breach of contract, fraud, fraud in the inducement, and unjust enrichment. They were claiming half of my equity interest, or 12.5 percent of the total, for their "vital real estate knowledge," and stated that both Jerry and I had promised them this percentage verbally. Moreover, they had a couple of witnesses, Roberto Bracho and Jeanette Faciolince (aka Gallegos, Luigi's wife), both of Doral Isles Real Estate (Fernandez Sr.'s company), who had filed affidavits that they had heard Jerry make these promises. The Fernandezes were demanding a jury trial.

This had the odd effect of renewing my loyalty to the Falwells. Jerry had threatened me in ways I found distasteful, and I was certainly ready to be done with both of them as soon as I could cash out my share. But with an outside threat, we were all on the same page again. It was us against the Fernandez clan, and once their lawsuit became a matter of public record, it was us against the media. Whatever residual bad feelings were in the air, we were going to have to set them aside for the time being.

I was not formally part of the lawsuit moving forward, as Resnick managed to have me removed as a defendant. Eventually, both Trey and Becki would be dismissed as well. Nor did I have to sit for depositions, which could have been far worse. But in the end, it didn't make much difference.

There were some odd turns along the way. For instance, at one point, we discovered that both father and son had changed their names. I found out about it when a Gordon Bello (aka Jesus Fernandez Jr.) tried to add a friend of mine to his new LinkedIn profile and the friend declined and informed me instead. I relayed the message to the Falwells and the rest of the legal team. Fernandez Sr. had been selectively using the alias Jett Bello—Bello being his wife's maiden name—going back at least to 2006. Under the Fernandez moniker, he had a bankruptcy case in which multiple creditors claimed he committed mortgage fraud. Tito settled on the alias Gordon Bello, most likely so he and his father could maintain their relationship as father and son. When he graduated from the University of Miami Law School in 2017, they both formally changed their names, in the middle of the lawsuit. This effectively shielded Fernandez Sr.'s former identity from undue attention.

Much of Fernandez Sr.'s dubious legacy was amassed in the run-up to the 2008 housing crisis and subsequent financial meltdown, Miami being the perfect petri dish for crooked bankers to offer subprime mortgages to hustler-operators without ethical guardrails, and where everyone can walk away when the game gets called. According to quotes from law enforcement I've seen specific to Florida, enough people there engage in mortgage and/or bankruptcy fraud that it's essentially too widespread to prosecute. In multiple cases, the senior Fernandez's creditors argued against his debt being retired through bankruptcy, alleging they were the product of fraud, like concealing mortgages in order to obtain new ones. "Jesus Fernandez" is among the most common names in any Latino-dominated culture—like John Smith in Anglo culture—and it likely afforded him the relative freedom of hiding in plain sight. This would've allowed him to operate with impunity for decades, and once the collective weight of his misdeeds became an undue burden, he could change his name and never look back.

As long as I've known him, "Gordon" wanted his friends to believe his father was a successful businessman, instead of the common hustler he really was. He grew up believing his family was rich, but his father merely accumulated millions in debt, which eventually imploded with predictable finality. I used to feel bad for them, and in the misguided enthusiasm of youth thought I could give them both a fresh start. But they have a transactional view of the world, and they see any kindness as an opportunity. They both later stated they changed their names because they had received threats and feared for their safety, but that was merely another dodge. I had cut Tito out of my life when I was twenty-one, months before the deal closed, and have not thought about him since unless I was forced to.

Meanwhile, free of any connection to his father's reputation, the newly minted Gordon Bello, armed with a local law degree, landed a job with the Miami-Dade Board of County Commissioners, and according to his LinkedIn page currently serves as managing partner of an outfit called 1 Government Advisors.

The Fernandez/Bello lawsuit might have remained unremarked upon—a private misunderstanding between business partners who disagreed as to the terms of their partnership, although their exact identities remained fluid—except the Ambrosino article had put Jerry Falwell Jr. and Miami on the media's radar.

On May 31, 2018, reporter Aram Roston, writing for the

website BuzzFeed, broke the story of my business relationship with the Falwells, the general circumstances of our meeting, and the lawsuit that had propelled us into print, which he linked to in his second paragraph. It claimed the lawsuit had been originally filed in 2015, dismissed, and then refiled in 2017 (not technically true; the first time was a bill of discovery), and mentions Trey and Rebecca Falwell as members of the corporation. But the liberal use of quotation marks throughout foregrounded the story he wanted to tell: "a 'friendly relationship' with the pool attendant" who "was 'offered a share' in the Alton Hostel venture"; "the evangelical 'indicated that he wanted to help Granda establish a new career and build a business.' " It listed my name and, more importantly, my age and former profession. As previously noted, this was indirectly the genesis of the dreaded pool boy meme. The Politico article, with its lurid chronicle of the Miami backdrop, was also linked.

There was no mention of racy photos (and wouldn't be for another year), but the story was greeted by universal head-scratching. It didn't make sense on the face of it, and it was overshadowed by an even bigger bombshell: citing "a high-ranking official at Liberty University," Roston claimed that "Trump's fixer Michael Cohen, who is now facing a federal criminal investigation, helped arrange Falwell Jr.'s endorsement of Trump in January 2016." This allegation had gone previously unreported, and was made doubly intriguing by a second blind source with knowledge of the Trump campaign, who stated that "Cohen was so confident in Falwell Jr.'s support that he and Trump assured others, well before Trump announced his candidacy, that Falwell Jr. would issue an endorsement."

The story ends with a callback to the embedded Liberty official: "The source familiar with Falwell's endorsement decision says that he is 'sure' Falwell discussed the Florida lawsuit with Cohen."

This was the story that made me a public figure and dragged me into the glare of the media spotlight, which has still not abated.

CHAPTER 16

LAST STAND AT LYNCHBURG

In the years since our real estate deal came together, Becki would constantly remind me how often she'd gone to bat for me. "Do you know who had your back?" she'd say. "Do you know who fought for you? You wouldn't have this opportunity if it wasn't for me." Anything, it seemed, to ratchet up the leverage. Coming in, it's implicit—*See what I can do for you?* And then once you're in it, suddenly it's a debt you can never repay. *Look what I did for you. You owe me.* You have become part of their lie.

The very first time I visited Liberty, they constantly coached me to say this to this person, don't say that to that person, pretend you're like this. They're consummate liars; their lifestyle demands it of them. And the longer you're around them, the better their lies sound, until finally you start to lie to yourself.

On August 6, 2018, Angelina and I had dinner with Jerry and Becki in Miami at Stiltsville Fish Bar, along with Caroline (who was now as tall as I was), her boyfriend, and a friend. Something happened there that I'm still deeply ashamed about. Before dinner, almost by force of habit, Jerry and Becki took me aside and told me I should ditch Angelina later and come have sex with them instead. I told them, once again, that things with my girlfriend were serious now, and I couldn't do that. But this time, during dinner, at 8:29 p.m., with her daughter and her daughter's friends right there at the table, Becki texted me the following: "Hey. You love amazing." (I'm sure that's supposed to be "look" amazing.) And then, "You missed out. I'm not wearing panties." This was the same dinner where, in front of everyone, they offered me a formal position managing the university's portfolio. I was flattered, but the timing was suspect, since they knew of my plans to attend graduate school in DC in the fall; Jerry even wrote me an effusive letter of recommendation. I told them I'd think about it, but I already had serious reservations.

After dinner, while we were getting the check, Becki texted me again at 9:37 p.m.: "You should give me and Jerry a ride." Double entendre or not, we did offer to drive everyone back to their hotel, but we all couldn't fit in the same car, so they ordered an Uber. While we were waiting, Jerry and Becki pressured me to drive them without the others, and so I asked Angelina if she would mind riding with Caroline and her friends in the Uber, even though she didn't really know any of them, and I knew it wasn't right to ask her. Reluctantly, she agreed. I drove, Becki rode shotgun, and Jerry was in the back, and as soon as we got on the road, Becki unzipped my jeans and went down on me, while Jerry recorded it all on his iPhone. I could have stopped her, but it had been a constant onslaught, and my resolve finally gave out. I felt like I had to. I was confused about everything, and paralyzed by my own feelings of a lack of self-worth, and I let it happen for a few minutes, before telling her to get away. I deeply regret being too weak to tell them no.

On my way home after dropping Becki and Jerry off at their hotel, I asked Angelina her opinion of the job offer Jerry made at dinner. In no uncertain terms, she told me she thought it was a terrible idea. Being that close to the both of them, in a city they owned, a one-company town where they could wield influence over both the municipal government and local constabulary? Look how demanding they were just flying down to Miami every other month. That wasn't a prospect; it was a trap. I agreed, and told her that my goal was to pivot away from the Falwells as quickly as I could, hopefully by securing an internship in the fall.

During dinner, Jerry had also mentioned that he and Hiltzik thought it might be a good idea if I wrote a letter in my own words debunking all the "conspiracy theories" out there, the so-called lies that had begun to permeate the popular press, and that would only grow more prolific and pungent as time passed. I was anxious to clear my name, even if clearing my name meant selling a false narrative to the press, i.e., my version of the Falwells' cover story to keep the real story at bay. That night at dinner, we also discussed the final wording, which I envisioned as a bylined column in a major publication. (Angelina, not privy to my true relationship with the Falwells, believed that the public intimations of an affair were unjust, and that by crafting a statement denying these allegations, I was striking a blow for truth.

She even helped me edit it. Such was the upside-down world I had tumbled into.)

Here is some of what I wrote:

I met the Falwell family—including their children— and several of their friends while they were staying at the Fontainebleau Hotel, where I was working as a pool attendant . . . They stayed there for several days, so I was able to chat with them multiple times and learned that aside from their work at Liberty University they were interested in real estate investment. I pitched to the Falwell family how great it would be for them to invest in Miami because of the booming real estate market here.

. . . They were interested in investing in Miami anyway, they needed a local partner, and I was the one who kept pushing the idea to them over numerous conversations. I have learned over time that they are generous people who take their roles as leaders of a university seriously and genuinely care about helping the young people they meet succeed in their professional careers. There is no salacious story behind us working together or them giving me a chance; they have helped many people besides myself professionally without fanfare and without asking for recognition or media attention. Also, while working together on the Miami real estate venture, they emphasized to me the importance of getting my college degree. With their help and encouragement, I decided to go back to school in Miami and received my bachelor's degree in finance from Florida International University.

With regard to the "private plane" incident—which

happened one time in July 2013—I was in Virginia visiting my ex-girlfriend for our anniversary because she had a summer internship there. My flight back to Miami was around the same time as the date the Falwells, their children, and their friends had rented a private plane to fly to Miami for vacation, so they told me to join their group rather than flying separately to the same city.

Finally, despite my nontraditional educational and career trajectory, I will be moving to [New York/DC] to complete my [master's program] and also stay geographically closer to my current girlfriend of more than three years . . .

No sooner had I texted them than I heard back from Becki: "You're an incredible writer!" When I explained that Angelina had helped me edit it, she added, "Excellent!! Really good! You guys make a great team and have a very bright future, I am convinced." I assumed that once it ran, I would be on the record and could refer all inquiring minds to my statement, so that I didn't have to worry about it anymore. But as the weeks and months rolled by, this failed to materialize. They assured me they were waiting for the right opportunity. But for the time being, they would really appreciate it if I wouldn't talk to the press.

Having gotten my BBA in finance from FIU in December 2016, I made plans to move to DC at the end of August, where I would attend graduate school at Georgetown University in real estate finance and development. I had worked all the way through, adding classes whenever I could, which meant I graduated at twenty-six and not twenty-two like most of my high school friends. Angelina had moved to Cambridge two months before to start graduate school, so there was really nothing tethering me to Miami any longer, other than a real estate deal I wished to be rid of.

I had always worked a job while pursuing my degree, and I thought DC might offer a host of internship or employment opportunities. But with the steady trickle of stories in the press, not quite about me yet, but also not that far away, I was concerned that as my profile rose, so would these stories in my Google listings. It was enough of a consideration that I contacted John Gauger. He explained to me the problem was that in order to push the negative content down, I would need to publish positive content to replace the negative. This is almost impossible for a private individual caught up in a scandal covered by major media outlets. Even if I could find reporters willing to say something nice about me—and there weren't any so far—articles published in major venues like BuzzFeed, Politico, or even the *Washington Post* or *New York Times*, if it came to that, would blot out everything else put together.

When the Falwells found out I was moving to DC, and that my sister and mother would be helping me, Jerry and Becki insisted we all come spend the weekend with them and stay in the guesthouse. Lynchburg is three and a half hours from Washington, so this would be our next-to-last stop.

My whole family had met the Falwells in 2014 when they visited me in Miami and we had dinner together at Macchialina. Afterward, Becki wrote my mother a couple of letters, artifacts of southern gentility: "What a joy it was to finally meet your beautiful and gracious family!" reads one. ". . . Like Jerry said, I don't think we had ever met anyone that we felt we already knew so well, and the more we talked, the more it seemed like we were old friends." My mother sent them some bottles of Sortilège, a liqueur made from Canadian whisky and maple syrup, and Becki wrote an effusive thank-you letter back, in between catching them up on their latest travels and the NCAA standings.

Saying a bittersweet goodbye to the roiling, redolent city of my birth, we loaded everything I owned into a large container that was transported from Miami to Washington, DC, in an 18-wheeler. Freed of the burden of possessions, it turned into a road trip for the three of us, and was actually a lot of fun. We spent one night in Savannah, Georgia, another in Charleston, South Carolina, finally arriving at the Falwells' farm on the night of the third day. I was really looking forward to a fresh start in a new city, and confident I could parlay my few contacts into a job quickly. On the drive up, my sister confided that she thought I had moved on from my relationship with Becki years ago, and that by this point we had settled into a weird kind of friendship; maybe I believed that myself.

Late on Saturday, August 25, we pulled up to the Falwells' front gate and I used the access code Becki had texted me. We didn't see them that night, since they were babysitting their granddaughter. The next morning we all went out for brunch and Jerry and Becki gave us a tour of the Liberty campus, which they were proud to show off.

I had my dog, Logan, with me, and as we were walking into a building, an employee ran up to stop us from entering with a dog, even though he was on a leash. Becki turned around and simply nodded, and the woman apologized profusely and returned to her desk. Another reminder that the beautiful, sculpted grounds and endowed architecture were all a part of their private kingdom.

We visited their daughter, Caroline, who was moving into

one of the dorms, and later went inner tubing on Snowflex, a dry, nonfreezing artificial snow, and then back to the house for drinks, followed by some four-wheeling along the trails on their five hundred acres. I also rode a Jet Ski on their private lake.

At one point, while we were showing my mom and sister the property, Jerry and Becki took me aside and encouraged me to find some time to slip away up to the house later so we could have sex. This time, I told them no. I had a girlfriend now, and they needed to respect that. This caught them off guard—especially after our recent Miami encounter. They had assumed everything was back to normal now; in retrospect, it's probably why they invited me to the farm in the first place. That night, my mother, sister, and I all turned in early, since we planned to leave bright and early the next morning. But as I was settling in at the guest-house, Becki texted me an excuse so I could come back up to the main house for a hug—her euphemism for sex.

Becki: Wi-Fi working?

(No answer from me.)

Becki: Hopefully you can come down by yourself later so we can hug goodbye . . . just hug. I was totally caught off guard.

Me: ;)

Becki: Well??? Will you? You can say you have to call Angelina.

Me: We shall see.

Me: You gotta earn it ;)

Becki: Please.

Me: I love you! DT [don't text]

("I was totally caught off guard" refers to my earlier rebuff.)

Eventually, just like the last time, I gave in. They were relentless, and in my diminished state, I felt somehow like I owed them. I vowed that this would be the last time.

Even though my relationship with Angelina looked perfect from the outside, things were rocky, and we had broken up two or three times in the recent past. Relocating to different cities while on different academic tracks—me to DC and graduate school, her to Cambridge to go to law school—was not helping. I secretly didn't think it was sustainable, and I wasn't convinced we were compatible to begin with. It seemed to me like a turning point, and that's always when your defenses drop and insidious ideas take hold. That was Becki. She was ruthless, and skilled in the art of seduction, or at least of exploiting a power differential to get what she wanted. I was adrift; I actually had no home. And so eventually she wore me down, and I did what she asked.

And then there were the videos. Beyond my own complicity and moral failings, there was the fact that the Falwells had half a dozen videos of Becki and me having sex, and those were just the ones I knew about. Aside from the embarrassment and chaos they could unleash, they also represented an unspoken form of blackmail, since implicitly, I had to do whatever they wanted. And what they wanted was to keep having sex. This eventually would reach a breaking point, and it turned out this was it. When our story finally went public, I said they had been blackmailing me the whole time, and I stand by that, even if they might not articulate it the same way. They always had these videos hanging over my head, and for every second of that time, I carried a gnawing fear in the pit of my stomach that this would be my downfall. It almost was.

I excused myself and went up to the house to use the Wi-Fi. Jerry and Becki both greeted me at the front door, and we walked to the living room. Becki closed the curtains so no one could see us, and within seconds, we were on the couch making out, and then quickly, having sex. Jerry was sitting in the recliner just to our left, and once again he filmed us on his iPhone. Then he began to masturbate.

After we finished, Becki seemed happy, and I was spent. I walked back down to the guesthouse, reflecting on what I'd done. I felt terrible, and angry, most of all with myself for sliding back into this position yet once again. *What's the worst that can happen?* seemed to be my motto at twenty. Now seven years later, and I had my answer. Or so I thought.

The guesthouse loomed before me. It was already way creepy in the best of times: a deconsecrated church, dating back to the nineteenth century, where it's always pitch-black outside at night. I went to sleep and reflected on my new life, which couldn't come soon enough. Then sometime between 2:00 and 3:00 a.m., there was a loud banging on the window. I woke up yelling from a deep sleep, in turn waking up my mom and sister. I went to the window and peered out, but there was no one there.

The next morning at breakfast, Jerry took me aside and confessed that it was him at the window: since both cell service and Wi-Fi were out, Becki had sent him down with an invitation to come back for round two. He said he ran away when I started shouting. He would have been pretty tanked up at that point in the evening, and he made a joke about it in front of everyone, but it fell flat. The whole breakfast was pretty awkward. I noticed my mother watching Becki, and she leaned over to me at one point and whispered, "She's being flirtatious with you." I couldn't argue with her.

When my family first learned of my true relationship with the Falwells, my sister found the whole thing repulsive—that Becki could carry on like this in full view of her children. My sister knew more than anybody else, because she's the one I'm closest to. And I told both my parents after the lawsuit came to light, because if they were going to hear it, I wanted them to hear it from me. My parents were shocked, mainly that the Falwells could do this. I remember my mother said, "You're the same age as their children!" I told my family I had stopped sleeping with Becki in 2015, when I got together with Angelina, which was true. But what none of them could see was the emotional relationship, which never really ended, and which apparently I was unable to quit. Now that it was pretty obvious I had relapsed, my sister couldn't wait to get out of there.

And yet for all that, my sister still remarks on how charming and present Becki was, and how she draws you in and disarms you: "She's instantly like your new best friend."

CHAPTER 17

AN ANGEL ON MY SHOULDER

I entered Georgetown University just as my personal life was becoming the stuff of public conjecture. I wasn't a public figure, hadn't grown up in a prominent family, and really wasn't prepared for that degree of attention suddenly directed squarely at what I had believed were my private concerns. I felt powerless, like I was in quicksand. Like everyone was laughing at me, and I was the last to know.

Literally one day into my new life, Jerry, Becki, and the whole gang showed up in DC. There was a dinner at the White House for a hundred of Trump's top evangelical advisers, of which the Falwells were among the most esteemed, so they all piled into the private jet and flew in for the day. There was an after-dinner event at the Trump Hotel that I attended as their guest, along with my mom and sister, who were still helping me set up my new apartment. I ran into Dr. Tim Clinton, who I had met when we were working on Gaming Detox, and Paula White, who had been at the 2012 Convocation, and her husband, Jonathan Cain, the keyboardist from Journey.

We also visited the Falwells' congressman Bob Goodlatte, a family friend, who took us on a tour of the Capitol rotunda. There, in the darkened interior, Becki tried to hold my hand. Maybe it was the element of risk she liked best about it. She couldn't help herself, but it spooked me and I jerked my hand away. Later, I saw Trey staring at us in a way he hadn't before— like he was suddenly suspicious of everything he thought he knew, or had been told.

When they got back to Lynchburg, Becki called and offered to buy me an engagement ring for Angelina. I had seen them do this with other young people in their inner circle, and I had the sense it was a valedictory offering, like I had graduated to a new plane in my relationship with them. Perhaps it's the same reason they offer people jobs, or find them investment opportunities. It's their exit strategy. Soon enough, Becki would grow tired of me and need a new diversion. If I was married, successfully employed, owed my fortune to them, or at least the gateway to one, then I would probably be more inclined to keep their secrets.

Or else maybe they would never give me up. Maybe they would come around whenever the desire drove them. Droit du seigneur and all that. (If you don't know what that means, I'm not going to be the one to tell you.) Was I supposed to still be doing this when I'm forty? Texting her "I love you" every night. Being her pillow to cry on. The whole thing was messing with my mind. Or else it was one more textbook ploy to stave off the inevitable. Either way, I told her thanks but no thanks.

And then, almost like clockwork, things went south with Angelina. On a trip she took down that first weekend, during which I had to study for a test, she felt like I hadn't paid enough attention to her and was upset that I didn't appear interested in exploring the city together. The tipping point came during the Brett Kavanaugh Supreme Court confirmation hearings the first week in September, when she called me in tears.

Like much of the nation, she had been watching them intensely, horrified at the prospect of the #MeToo movement now being exposed in the loftiest reaches of our government. She had watched Kavanaugh accuser Christine Blasey Ford's testimony, and the hostility apparent in the questions directed at her, and she couldn't understand why we were having this debate over bad behavior that should have been considered beyond the pale. Moreover, she couldn't understand the appeal to me of these Trump enablers and probable racists I seemed to be in cahoots with, or this weird loyalty I had toward them. Nor did I seem particularly interested in engaging on the topic of predatory sexual behavior, which she mistook for apathy on my part, and not something darker and closer to home. This was just as the Florida lawsuit was circling back around, and there was this invisible creature she couldn't have known about—because I'd never told her—always chewing at the edges of the frame. It was all starting to take a silent toll on my mental health. She kept pushing me to explain it to her, culminating in the moment I finally broke down and kept repeating "I want to die" over and over again. We broke up soon after.

Alone in a new and daunting environment, facing intellectual and financial challenges the likes of which I had never experienced, my anchor and soul mate suddenly a phantom memory, no job to keep my mind occupied, no way to cash out my investments, unseen forces lurking somewhere in the distance, with my darkest secret just about to crawl out into the light, I was soon staring into the face of a pretty major depression. Given my circumstances, the only one I could really talk to about it was Becki. And the more depressed I got, the more Becki reached out to catch me as I was falling. Here's a typical text thread from November 29, 2018:

Me: I don't care anymore.

Becki: That's not true.

Me: Our relationship and my reputation was ruined.

Me: Goodnight.

Becki: Two days ago it was fine and you were telling me about [a girl I had started dating]. What happened?

Me: Sometimes I wished I never bumped into you guys at the Fontainebleau.

Becki: We are happy about you and your new friend.

Me: It crushes me every time I Google my name and read the articles.

Me: It's always going to be there.

Becki: No it won't. Jerry is working on the business article.

Me: Yeah, but those articles will always be there.

Me: They have been read several times.

Becki: The closing took a long time and you just need to let us work on this.

Me: I'm not going to text anymore. Goodnight.

Becki: Ok. Let's talk on the phone.

Me: No.

Me: Goodnight.

Becki: I love you!

Becki: Why can't we just talk?

The line about "you just need to let us work on this" seemed to be a reference to Hiltzik, who she had confided earlier was helping them manage the stories in the press. Here and later, she would encourage me to vent to her whenever I wanted—to get it off my chest, "no judgment." She assured me that she and Jerry weren't the enemy, but rather a safe outlet to voice my frustrations. It was the maternal side of Becki, buffed up to a high sheen. What I didn't know was that she was doing the same thing with my ex-girlfriend after our breakup: *Oh my God, is everything okay? What is he telling you? You can vent to me, I know he can be a real asshole at times . . . I thought you guys were going to get married.* Reams of this stuff. At one point soon after our breakup, still angry at me, Angelina told her, "He's such a racist! Can you imagine what he'd say about my family?" As a fellow child of immigrants, she had been rightly troubled by Jerry's comments about Muslims, and couldn't understand why I would give him the benefit of the doubt—all of which she was now recycling for the benefit of Jerry's wife. She later apologized to me about it.

Becki also tried to reach out to my sister, noting that I was upset, and asking her, "Are we still friends?" My sister told her, "Of course he's upset. His life is fucking ruined!" But Becki didn't stop there: that winter is when I started dating Hailey, a woman I met at Georgetown (again, not her real name). After the whole story came out and the Falwells and I were now enemies, Becki started texting Hailey, too. She sabotaged the relationship to such an extent that we finally had to break up in early 2021. Her family didn't want to get dragged into any of this, and I agreed that they shouldn't. It was tough for us to break it off, because we really didn't want to, but she wanted no part of this, and I can't blame her.

I told myself Becki has a volcanic jealousy somewhere beneath the den mother image she tries to project and her sex bomb persona ticking right below the surface. And that she was constantly planting seeds of doubt between me and my girlfriends because she wanted me all to herself. But I don't think that really does her justice.

A ten-thousand-word profile on the Falwells appeared in the March 2022 issue of *Vanity Fair*. Written by Gabriel Sherman, it is largely sympathetic to their plight and perceived fall from grace. Their PR team's fingerprints are all over it: Jerry concedes Becki's "affair" but passionately denies his own participation. He charges me with extortion, naming me as the culprit who "shared—or sold" the photos. He blames his testosterone intake (to tone himself up physically in the wake of Becki's indiscretion) as responsible for his less defensible public behavior, and his persistent health problems for not fighting back against me in the press or the Liberty board when it moved to strip him of his power (conveniently ignoring his behind-the-scenes efforts in both). Large swaths of the article detail Jerry's struggles against the legacy of his father, and to forge his own religious identity. Becki makes this tale of Jerry's forty days in the wilderness explicit in the story's final line, thus completing their long-standing fallback plan of throwing her under the bus to preserve his legacy: " 'We're together more than any couple you will ever meet in your life,' Becki said, as she sat on a stool at the kitchen island. 'He forgave me, and that's what Jesus teaches, forgiveness.' "

She conveniently sidesteps reports of other infidelities, including one with a Liberty student. More recently, it was announced that a miniseries will be made based on the article, no doubt preserving their burnished version of the truth in amber.

But all of this pales in comparison to Becki's version of the events at their farm in late August 2018. Here is the excerpt:

When Granda drove from Miami to Washington, D.C., in late August 2018, Jerry even offered to let Granda, his mom, and his sister stay on the farm to break up the trip.

Jerry and Becki hoped it would be a chance to wish Granda goodbye. But according to Jerry and Becki, the visit took a harrowing turn.

The morning after Granda and his family arrived at the farm, Becki said Granda texted her that the Wi-Fi in the guesthouse wasn't working. Becki said moments later, she found Granda in her daughter Caroline's bedroom. He explained he wanted to stay there because there was internet service. Becki said the next thing she knew, Granda pushed her onto the bed. They hadn't slept together since 2014, she said, and she didn't want to start again. "He said he wanted to have sex and I said, 'No, no, no,' " Becki recalled. Jerry was in the shower down the hall and couldn't hear what was happening. Becki said Granda kept pressuring her. "I kept saying no. I didn't want to do it. But I was scared to death of him too, because he was still holding everything over me, so we had sex." Becki said it was over quickly. "He left and I went into the room and just cried." (Again, when asked to comment on the specifics of this magazine piece, Granda issued a blanket denial.)

Becki said she didn't report the traumatic experience at the time because she felt guilty about the affair. In her mind, she deserved it. A few months later, Becki told Jerry and two lawyers about the incident. Becki said it also took her time to process that what happened could have been a form of assault. "I said no. Just because we had sex before does not mean he has a free ticket to my body."

Outside of a blanket denial, I had refused to cooperate with the story because of this book and an upcoming documentary.

I referred the author to a 2020 article by Josh Kovensky on the political website Talking Points Memo, which includes details of my weekend at the Falwells' farm (conveniently excluded from the article).

I have time-stamped copies of our texts, and our last tryst took place in the early evening, not the morning. My mother and sister can attest to Jerry's late-night trip to the guesthouse, and I will testify under oath to all of the above, if and when the time is appropriate. Subsequent events, detailed in the remaining chapters, belie her claims in stark, bold relief. But my question is this:

What kind of person would capitalize on the #MeToo movement, the long-awaited reckoning of privileged male behavior, the fall of once invincible titans like Harvey Weinstein and countless others, to make false accusations, just to save her own skin? To offer up a diversion and a smokescreen to protect her own hypocritical lifestyle? Especially when they know, and they know I know, there's video of the act in question?

A cornered and desperate person, perhaps. Someone so clueless and detached from the world around them that they can't see the sea change that soon will overtake them. Or what I suspect is the truest answer:

A sociopath.

CHAPTER 18

RIDE THE WHIRLWIND

Around December 2018, Aram Roston, now of Reuters partly on the strength of the story he had broken about us in BuzzFeed, reached out to Jerry about Becki's nude photos, our trip to Cheeca, Michael Cohen, and Donald Trump. He had been doing his research. Based on what he was hearing from the Bellos (the Fernandezes), as telegraphed in their lawsuit, he thought there might be a sexual relationship between Jerry and me. He was also interested in whether Michael Cohen had blackmailed Jerry to secure his endorsement of Trump, which would have been a crime—not to mention banner headlines. Privately, Jerry attributed the Bellos' escalating rhetoric to the fact that he had filed a motion to dismiss their lawsuit, and they were getting antsy watching their ship coming in, only to see it get blown off course by gale-force winds.

The Bellos would lose their leverage if details of the photos leaked out, since actually releasing them would have been extortion. The only sway they held over Jerry and Becki was the threat to confirm the existence of the photos. As I mentioned, the lawsuit was a delivery mechanism for discovery, and discovery meant they could ask anyone about anything. This is what keeps people with secrets up at night. But the Falwells hadn't sustained any lasting damage yet, never mind the dark clouds of rumor circling overhead. From their vantage point, if Roston was getting bad information, and if other reporters weren't following his lead yet, that put him where Woodward and Bernstein were in the early days of Watergate—way out ahead of the pack, with some serious people assuring him he was headed in the wrong direction. The Falwells were friendly with Sean Hannity, Jeanine Pirro, and many of the Fox on-air personalities—Becki used to brag that Hannity texted her during the commercial breaks—and nobody over there had taken an interest. Jerry's feeling was that conservatives see so much garbage on social media as a matter of course that they're already in a defensive crouch and reject it all. It still seemed to them like things might blow over.

At the direction of their PR and legal teams, they put together a joint strategy to make sure we were all on the same page. In their meeting with me in December, Jerry reiterated what his lawyer, Woody Fowler, chairman and CEO of Williams Mullen, the third-largest law firm in Virginia, had told him when they started: No matter what questions the reporter asks, just stick to the script, 100 percent. A call was scheduled January 7, 2019, between Jerry and Woody in Virginia, and Roston and his

Reuters editors in Washington, DC, and London. The ground rules would be that Jerry's remarks would be off the record, and he would approve quotes after the fact on an individual basis, which Roston agreed to. Jerry's argument, as spelled out in the run-through, was that bad actors (the Bellos), both clueless (they thought the Cheeca photos were from the Caribbean) and flailing (Jerry and I were homosexual lovers, Michael Cohen had threatened Jerry for his endorsement—presented as equally risible), had inverted the truth, and now Reuters was carrying their water.

Moreover, the lawsuit was a shakedown, their witnesses were shills (we had never met any of them), and the mediation had been handled badly. Jerry would hammer all that home with the sentiment, "I can tell you they don't have what they're telling you they have." According to him, Hiltzik assured him it was all going to work out fine. In addition, Jerry's position on the lawsuit itself was: If you're claiming 12.5 percent of the deal, then take it—we'll take it out of Becki's half, and then we're done. It's barely worth what's owed on it anyway. (Meaning then, not now.) Either way, whether it was shut down or settled, their lawsuit was on thin ice.

The conference call with Roston et al. followed this script pretty carefully, interspersed with long discursions on Jerry's background and the way he got started. These experiences he had attempted to pay forward to me (as a way of explaining my place in all this). He was my friend and mentor; I was ambitious, reminded him of himself starting out, and he liked that I had skin in the game. The Cheeca trip consisted of me driving up to discuss business face-to-face with them, in surroundings to which they were accustomed. Any rumored sex photo or evidence of sexual misconduct was inconceivable. And despite what the "conspiracy theorists" want you to believe, he was friends with Michael Cohen *and* a committed Trump supporter. And nobody told him what to do because no one ever tells him what to do. The Reuters team agreed to take all of this under advisement.

My family could sense I was under a lot of pressure and had been after me to see a therapist, but the few sessions I went to, I was too paranoid to open up about the actual source of my problems. Meanwhile, this sub-rosa black ops campaign against me, or whatever it was, had hit a flash point with the gun incident in the Taco Bell parking lot, gone dormant after the election, and then resumed a year earlier in DC. It had also lost all pretense of being undercover: SUVs rolled by my apartment at all hours, the drivers glaring at me as they passed. When I took an Uber to class, a surveillance vehicle screeched to a halt inches behind us. I'd try and lose a tail in traffic, making ridiculous hairpin turns, and they always stayed right with me. Later on, Hailey and I were jogging on a park trail and two guys started following us who could not have looked less like joggers, and who didn't lose us no matter what. Another time, Hailey couldn't get me on the phone for a couple of hours when I was taking a nap and called my sister in tears, convinced something terrible had happened to me. This kind of thing happened so often I was starting to recognize the same drivers in different cars. When I told my lawyer and others about it, they thought I was being hysterical.

To add to the growing mix, I needed to work to pay my way through school, yet every job interview I went on, the first thing people would do was Google my name, where they would come across one of the half dozen articles in reputable news outlets tying me into this demented sex-adjacent political scandal that wasn't quite a scandal yet. They didn't begin to understand it, but this was Washington, the seat of government and power, so they knew enough at least to keep as far away from it as they could get.

Then on Tuesday, January 15, 2019, at 11:47 p.m., after she and Jerry had been out at some function, Becki FaceTimed me. She was a little tipsy, slurring her words slightly. And she was naked, with a flirtatious leer. And I did something I might not have thought to do before. I pressed the record button on my iPhone. There's no sound recorded, a built-in security feature. But for the next seven minutes and three seconds, she takes me on a walking tour of their house, in and out of focus, occasionally sipping a glass of white wine. She stops in practically every room, but I'm the only one who would understand the significance: This is every location where we had sex over the course of our seven-year illicit romance: the family antiques and game room, the guest room, one of the kids' bedrooms, the bed swing on the balcony off the master bedroom, the kitchen island, the couch in the living room. Periodically, she stops and focuses the camera on her breasts so that they fill the frame. One time she pans down to her vagina and holds. Jerry follows along behind her throughout, intermittently visible peeking around a bedroom door or framed in a stairway, wearing his implacable Cheshire cat smile, and possibly more than a little lit. "Remember this?" it looks like she's saying. "Remember that time?"

In one bedroom, she lies down on her back and spreads her legs. As she approaches the front door, I can see her underwear and evening clothes strewn about where she let them fall. Now she's putting on her panties, doing a reverse striptease. There is a date and time stamp, and a running clock throughout. All the while, I can see myself as a floating head in the small box at the top of the screen, with a sickly pasted-on smile that never changes, while my eyes flicker and dart around and I grow increasingly incapable of a casual response. This was four and a half months after my last trip to Lynchburg, where she says I sexually assaulted her.

The next day, Becki reached out on my behalf to John Regan at Permanens Capital, the investment firm that handles the university's war chest, to ask about finding me a job in Washington. An ask that would go exactly nowhere, just circle around on itself like a dust devil of possibility, using up more time, more hope, more lost opportunity that was never mine in the first place.

If I had to bet, I'd say Becki thought this garish display would trip something inside of me, and I would invite them to DC for the weekend. Then they'd have a foothold, and they could see where it goes, maybe set things right.

Five days after that, on January 20, as if I wasn't on edge already, Becki texted me screenshots of texts she'd received of what was clearly a death threat to her and her family. Here are the texts in their uncorrected state:

"Hello // I have an important information for you // Good Day, I want you to read this message very crefully, and keep the secret with you till further notice, You have no need of knowing who i am, where am from, till i make out a space for us to see, i have being paid $20,000.00 in adbance to terminate you with some reasons listed to me by my employer, its one i believe you call a friend, i have followed you closely for one week and three days now and have seen that you are innocent of the accusation,

Do not contact the police or F.B.I or try to send a copy of this to them, because if you do i will know, and might be pushed to do what i have being paid to do, beside this is the first time i turned out to be a betrayer in my job."

The texts were accompanied by a recent photo of Jerry and Becki with their granddaughter, and a second photo of a pistol aimed at the camera with the caption, "You got 10 hours to live."

I texted her back immediately, and she wrote: "Obviously someone trying to scare me and has done research." She said they actually had police sleeping at their house, and that the matter was being investigated by the Bedford police, Virginia State Police, and the FBI. No account of it ever appeared in the press or any of their legal documents that I'm aware of, and it happened to occur within three days of news reports that Michael Cohen, now sentenced to three years in prison beginning in May, had canceled his testimony before the House Committee on Oversight due to what he claimed were "death threats" coming from Trump and his attorney Rudy Giuliani. To be fair, both Trump and Giuliani—on Fox and CNN, respectively—called for Cohen's wife and father-in-law to be investigated, and then a wave of death threats poured in from Trump supporters.

This all seems very cloak-and-dagger on the face of it, if not borderline absurd. But Ronan Farrow, in his book *Catch and Kill*, claimed the Israeli private intelligence company Black Cube was hired by Harvey Weinstein in the summer of 2017 to track down and presumably dissuade journalists from running problematic stories. Eventually, one of the agents, a Ukrainian who was subcontracted through the PI firm InfoTactic, confessed to Farrow of his work for Black Cube: "I fear that it may be illegal." In Julie K. Brown's book *Perversion of Justice: The Jeffrey Epstein*

Story, the *Miami Herald* reporter notes that when writing her story about the Falwells and our rendezvous at Cheeca Lodge, her colleague on the story, Doug Hanks, claimed his source told him that "a man with a thick New York accent had called and threatened to harm him if he didn't keep quiet about the naughty pictures." Elsewhere in the book, the tactics she describes were very familiar to me: random delivery guys knocking on the door despite not having ordered anything, or trying the door to see if it was open. I once asked one of these guys what he wanted, and he walked away without saying anything.

In February, I applied for a coveted internship at a real estate consulting firm and went through multiple rounds of interviews. They had plenty of opportunities to shut me down, but they seemed to like me, and I was eventually offered the internship, which I accepted. When I expressed my excitement to Becki and Jerry over the phone, they asked me the name of the company. Almost as soon as I told them, the job offer was rescinded. For the record, I have no idea why the company didn't hire me. I can only present it as another in a series of inexplicable coincidences. But in retrospect, it was a breaking point. I remember talking to a reporter around that time and trying to feed him the official story, off the record, and he said, "You're fucked, man. You're going to have to change your name."

CHAPTER 19

THE REAL POOL BOY

In the end, Reuters blinked and backed off the rumored sex angle. Their story ran on May 7, and like almost every other paper in the country, focused on the transcripts of a phone call between Michael Cohen—supposedly speaking candidly and confidentially, although guys like that never do or say anything that isn't thought out beforehand—and comedian Tom Arnold, of all people, who secretly recorded it and released clips of it into the wild on April 24 via a story in the *Wall Street Journal*, which posted the clips on their website. Arnold has had kind things to say about me, beginning with the *Gangster Capitalism* podcast, where he claimed: "In my opinion, out of all this—Trump, Jerry Falwell Jr., all their people, and even Michael Cohen—the person who comes out of this standing tall, all of this, is Giancarlo Granda. This kid, he's the hero to me." Arnold has also been around the block, and no doubt understood at the time that he was being used to shape a preconceived narrative. And central to Cohen's argument was me.

The pool boy.

Over time, I've become desensitized to the "pool boy" label, and see it as a way for my handful of enemies to dehumanize and degrade me, and everyone else to have a little fun at my expense. People mean well, but the name itself is like a stake through my heart. Do a quick audit of your own life: What was your first job? Where did you work when you were twenty? Flipping burgers at McDonald's? As a lifeguard during summer break? Barback at Chili's? Now freeze that moment in amber and imagine this is what you'll be called well into your adult life. Suddenly the laziest daily columnists or talk show hosts can't resist the urge to turn you into a punch line, and it's what strangers call you when they recognize you.

By the time Cohen's book was published in 2020, the term was already in wide use. It's there in the headline of that first BuzzFeed article by Aram Roston, although they softened it editorially to "Young Pool Attendant." It gets shortened to "pool boy" in a tweet by Roston on the same day, syndicated in the *Daily Mail* that evening, and then was picked up by the Twitter hive in the hours afterward to spread forth into the world. Tom Arnold was one of those on Twitter, right then on a public jihad against Donald Trump, which sent him on a quixotic odyssey to contact Michael Cohen, then me, and then Gordon Bello in the hopes that one of these target-rich tributaries would hold the secret weapon to take down his bête noire.

Arnold is one of those guys for whom Twitter is like a million tiny arrows. Through 2018 and into 2019, he produced half a dozen tweets that referred to me by that name (that largely defended me), including one in December 2018 accusing Cohen of facilitating the "millions" the Falwells paid me prior to the election. (As if.) "If Michael Cohen wants to show America he's really changed he'll acknowledge this," he wrote, thus ensuring it would come to the fixer-in-chief's attention. (However improbable, Arnold also played himself in a 2011 "comedy" called *The Pool Boys*, which might be why the epithet came readily to mind.) His goading finally got Cohen to call him on March 25, 2019, the full tape of which Arnold sat on until May 7, the day after Cohen entered prison, when he provided it to Roston. In it, Cohen attempts to set the record straight on the version of Jerry Falwell Jr.'s slow-motion fall from grace that Arnold had been promoting on his Twitter feed.

After whining that the Falwells no longer speak to him ("who I brought to the table"), Cohen launched into the matter at hand. "The reason why I called you [is], if there's an error in something, they [the media] come after you hard. Me as well. We're held to a different standard . . . The story that you're talking about with Jerry? It's not accurate. Nowhere close to accurate. That's not what it's about. That's not what I spoke to the pool boy, or whatever he is [about] . . . Really it has nothing to do with Jerry having relations with the pool boy and so on." When Tom Arnold brings up Becki, Cohen says, "Well, she didn't have sex with the pool boy either."

Instead, he suggests, it was merely "a bunch of photographs, personal photographs" that the Falwells had taken and wished to keep secret. "I actually have one of the photos," he says, in a ready-made sound bite that set Twitter on fire. "It's terrible." Cohen explains that he planned to broker a financial settlement, but "it never happened. The guy just either deleted them on his own, or what have you."

"And that's why I reached out," he offers in closing. "Because it's happened to a couple of people who I know, who are the wives of celebrities. And when their phones get hacked, and they have private photos of themselves—they're not ever used to that. And, you know, she has a very nice figure. And nobody wants their private photos out there—especially when you have children and grandchildren . . . So, my heart went out to Becki. And you know, I loved them. They were like family to me. And now I don't speak to them."

It's all there. The tough-guy lawyer appealing to standards of honor and decency. The humblebragging insider as confidant to his showbiz pals and their randy wives. The champion of moral dignity, in the most delicate terms possible, telling you he's gotten a peek at the damaged goods. All in that suggestive manner favored by mobsters to uncouple threats from agency. But the most interesting thing, if you actually listen to him speaking and not simply read the transcript, is how effortlessly he lies.

Alongside Aram Roston at Reuters, Arnold also released the phone call in its entirety, apparently because they asked for it, to the TBS comedy news series *Full Frontal with Samantha Bee.*

In a nine-and-a-half-minute comedy segment airing on August 14, 2019, under the heading, "The Case of Jerry Falwell Jr., the Pool Boy, Michael Cohen & Tom Arnold," some variation of the term "pool boy" ("pool guy," "pool man," "pool attendant") appears an excruciating twenty times—in Bee's

monologue, inset newspaper headlines, and recurring graph-
ics, including one that reads "Did Somebody F**k the Pool
Guy?" (It also gets off at least one great line: "Jerry Falwell Jr.
is the son of the late televangelist and stealer of Pee-wee Her-
man's bike Jerry Falwell Sr.") It's true that Tom Arnold comes
off as a clown, which is collateral damage for his troubles. But
Tom Arnold is a career comedian with a five-year stint on one
of the most popular sitcoms of all time. In his world, that's a
win-win.

Arnold himself harbors no illusion about being used. "He
really was trying to give me misinformation," he says after the
fact. "That was his thing. He wanted me to stop with Falwell. I
mean, I was using him too, but he wanted a message out."

Except that Cohen didn't really need to convince Tom Arnold
of anything. He knew that Arnold was a wild card, a comedian,
a gadfly, not a journalist. He had every reason to anticipate that
Arnold would tape the call, and then leak it to the media the first
chance he got, probably after Cohen's sails were trimmed and his
power sapped. Michael Cohen had been sentenced to prison in
mid-December and disbarred by the New York State Supreme
Court by late February. He probably already planned to write a
tell-all memoir in prison, meaning his one money client would
be dead to him moving forward. The Falwells were the only ar-
rivistes in that world potentially willing to pay for his skills as
a tour guide, and they were no longer speaking to him. He had
to roll the dice while he was still the shooter. And he had every
reason to believe I wouldn't come forward to challenge him. The
media vacuum would do the rest.

I would suggest that the disinformation was beside the
point. It reads more like a veiled message to the Falwells them-

selves, a proof of concept on his skills and a performative public statement of his loyalty to "a friend of ours," like the mob guys say in the movies, especially one who might still have Donald Trump's ear. And it likely worked; Jerry told me he and Cohen had dinner three days before Cohen entered prison, which he later claimed in the *Vanity Fair* story, and both Falwells certainly come off well in Cohen's book. Arnold claims he later prevailed upon Cohen to take up my cause—i.e., see to it that I was made whole in this business deal with his friends the Falwells—as a form of penance. Zen-like, Cohen texted back, "We're on different journeys," effectively severing ties between them for the last time.

One other curious detail I'd like to point out: Based on the evidence in his book, you would have to conclude that Cohen started out as a pool boy just like me. Summers during high school growing up in the Five Towns area of Long Island, he worked at his uncle Morty's "swanky catering hall and mob hangout" in Brooklyn, the El Caribe, flipping burgers and sucking up to the made men of the Lucchese and Gambino crews. "I was like the young Henry Hill character in *Goodfellas*," he writes, "fetching drinks and lighting cigarettes for the Lucchese crime family—which was actually the exact crew that hung out at the El Caribe and was fictionalized in Scorsese's movie." There he watched the wiseguys swim laps, work on their biceps, and plot murders, giddy with the proximity: "I was right in the middle of it," he writes, still incredulous at the prospect. In breathless prose, he recounts the menacing character in a white tank top who shoots a pool guest in the buttocks for sunbathing naked, how it was his responsibility to get the women and children out of the pool, and how a guy showed up two days later with an envelope full of $500 in twenties—the inciting incident in his own would-be life of crime.

Seen against this backdrop, his insistent use of the phrase seems to me a lot more like projection. For the record, Michael Cohen is the real pool boy.

Now go home and get your shine box.

CHAPTER 20

LIGHT THE MATCH

On May 8, 2019, the day after the Aram Roston article dropped on Reuters, *New Times Miami* ran a story with the headline, "Ex-Miami Beach Pool Attendant Denies Knowing Anything About 'Racy' Falwell Photos." In my interview for the story, I toed the company line and denied everything. When it posted online, I texted Jerry, "I really hope that you see this article as a sign of good faith, and that I will fulfill any conditions that are expected of me when we structure a buyout." I made sure he knew that included testifying against Gordon Bello, which it would be a pleasure to do. I reiterated that I needed to start investing on my own, media coverage had precluded me from achieving gainful employment, and the buyout he had long promised me was the solution to both. He seemed to agree, and told me, "I remember you saying many times that we'd be friends for life. I always believed you." I still thought we had a clear exit ramp to disentangle our lives amicably.

Jerry finally settled the Bellos lawsuit in October 2019. The amount is sealed by the court. Whatever they ended up getting, I wish them luck. I can't help but think that if Jerry had settled with me at the same time, his life might be very different today. Once he bought the Bellos out, there were no more hurdles left. Maybe we weren't on great terms at that point, and I'd said a lot of things in our heated text exchanges that I regret, and I would take back if I could. But I should have been an anecdote in the sweep of their lives, not the anchor they got tangled up in. If I had sued them under false pretenses like the Bellos did, I still would have walked away with something. They could have written me a check for one-quarter of the market value and owned it free and clear, a stake on the gold coast of an impending land boom.

But they didn't.

Gordon Bello did not go gently into the good night either, it turns out. As the story gathered momentum and more and more outrages came to light, he claimed he'd had a separate friendship with Jerry, unbeknownst to everyone else. Jerry took him and his friends to baseball games, bestowed on him some of that mentorship and guidance he'd lavished on me in the beginning, probably became the father that Gordon always wanted and never got. As media attention briefly swung around his way, he claimed he and Becki had enjoyed a "personal relationship" as well, Perhaps he needed a credible reason why he was in possession of naked photographs of her, and in his addled logic, that dictated that it should have been him instead of me. I wish it had been.

He was quoted in a May 2021 episode of the *Gangster Capitalism* podcast on the Falwells (in a phone call with recurring character Tom Arnold). Bello alleged he'd had an affair with Becki, one he somehow kept secret from his longtime girlfriend, and to which Becki and I were the only witnesses. On May 24, after the episode ran, Becki texted me, "Why is your friend saying that I had a 'relationship' with him? What is y'all's angle! You know that's a lie . . ." So in Becki's defense, let me be the one to say he's not my friend, and he made it all up out of whole cloth. Becki was right. It's a lie.

Throughout this gathering storm of media attention and the final events that would determine our fate, Becki was still texting me: "I get worried when I don't hear from you. Is everything OK?" Or sending me pictures of the Greek islands from the deck of somebody else's yacht. Meanwhile, I was trying to keep the wolf from the door. Since long before the settlement, there had been a constant stream of overtures on our part to get this matter resolved, and Jerry had always seemed amenable, save for this one insurmountable obstacle. Lawyer Woody Fowler had made it clear to my attorney that as soon as the lawsuit was settled, Jerry would buy me out. Since it no longer exerted a gravitational pull on our circumstances, I was anxious to get that process started. At one point, things got so challenging for me that I even reached out to Hiltzik, my one and only phone call with him, in the hopes that his vast network of contacts might find me meager employment. He assured me his people could suppress any negative Google results to the second page, which is the equivalent of digital Siberia, and my reputational challenges would go away. They knew people at investment companies, and they could help me get work there. Everything was going to be fine. It was all lovely to hear in the moment, and made me feel much better. And that's the last time I spoke with Matthew Hiltzik.

In mid-January 2020, I contacted attorney Lin Wood, then considered one of the premier defamation lawyers in the country, about the possibility of suing some of these media outlets for defamation, since everything they had reported about me so far had been innuendo. Wood had been the lead attorney in the Covington case, which involved a Catholic high school student who got in an ideological brawl at the Lincoln Monument and then sued the *Washington Post* and CNN to reach a settlement. Before that Wood had represented Richard Jewell, the security guard hero turned accused bomber of the 1996 Summer Olympics in Atlanta. Wood called me back and asked me if evidence would surface during discovery. I told him yes. He said there was a good chance I could prevail, but subsequent news coverage would focus on the embarrassing details, which would further feed the media monster, with the takeaway being the opposite of what I wanted. So I stood down. A year later, he would lose his mind to the QAnon cult.

By March, I felt I was running out of options. When Trey texted me a routine request, I told him to talk to my lawyer—specifically, to have Jerry contact Aaron Resnick and initiate talks about a buyout. There had never been friction between Trey and me before, and this marked a new wrinkle in our business relationship, my frustrations with Jerry and Becki now spilling over to the partnership at large. Wishing to be proactive, I sent Jerry a contract with the figures that he had given me in 2016 based on

Trey's calculations—$600,000 for each of us—in the hopes of jump-starting negotiations. As an alternative, Jerry had offered a La Quinta equity stake that would pay out $50,000 a year for twenty years, so those are the terms we included.

But in the weeks and months that followed, as one excuse after another landed in my path, my frustration level was reaching a boiling point. I could have sold my equity stake to a third party at any time, free and clear. This included any number of my business professors at Georgetown who had come out of the Washington establishment and were affiliated with hedge funds and the like. A $600,000 investment in a property this size would have struck a few of them as a good investment, and after Trump was elected president in 2016, the chance to be in business with one of his closest allies would have proved irresistible to some. But Jerry didn't want third parties in the LLC. As he told me ad nauseum, he wanted to retain family control.

While I struggled to escape the Falwells, Jerry was busy with other problems, too. Regardless of the private positions he had taken with me, in public Jerry remained unrepentant for his antediluvian attitudes on race. In January, he and Jim Justice, the governor of neighboring West Virginia, urged those counties in rural Virginia unhappy with the state's Democratic governor (Ralph Northam), two Democratic senators, and apparent permanent leftward tilt in state and national politics, to secede and join West Virginia.

Then one day after the murder of George Floyd by active-duty police officer Derek Chauvin in Minneapolis on May 25, 2020, the Bedford County Board of Supervisors (incorporating Lynchburg's western border) passed a resolution officially recognizing a local paramilitary militia. This followed a similar resolution by adjacent Campbell County, immediately to Lynchburg's south, the only two such actions taken nationally. Although the resolutions were not legally binding, they did serve to bestow an air of legitimacy on white nationalist militias amid national protests and rising public awareness of the Black Lives Matter movement.

The next day, Jerry thought it an appropriate time to reflect on the recently imposed statewide COVID mask mandate by posting an image on Twitter of himself wearing a mask emblazoned with a recently surfaced medical school yearbook photo of a student in blackface and another in a Klan robe, one of which was rumored to be Governor Northam. Northam himself never seemed clear as to whether he was depicted in the photo or not, although he eventually chose to apologize anyway. But not Jerry—who refused to apologize *or* to take down the tweet, referred to Northam as "Governor Blackface," and hawked the masks on conservative talk radio, inspiring staff and faculty resignations, and eventually a petition signed by 37,000 people telling him to stop. Twelve days later, Jerry finally issued an "apology" in which he blamed "the governor's racist past" and his insensitivity in reflecting on it.

But not before the owner of Fifth & Federal Station, a local whiskey bar and barbecue joint, tweeted his approval of Jerry's photo and protesters converged on the restaurant. Both local militias showed up in force, outweighing the police presence, and taking up sniper positions on adjacent rooftops. When apparent shots rang out, a melee ensued in which police sprayed the crowd with tear gas—although it was later determined the shots were actually fireworks. This in a city with a rich African American intellectual tradition. Anne Spencer, a widely respected African American poet, and one of the premier voices of the Harlem Renaissance of the twenties and thirties was a longtime resident of Lynchburg—her son Chauncey was one of Carey Falwell's top moonshine runners—and dignitaries such as Langston Hughes, Paul Robeson, and Martin Luther King Jr. were frequent weekend guests.

In a June 2020 text exchange, in the form of a final ultimatum, I told Jerry, "Since you're okay with ruining my life, I am going to take the kamikaze route. It really is a shame because I wanted to reach a peaceful resolution and just move on with our lives, but if conflict is what you want, then so be it." I would make good on my warnings that I would "clear it up with reporters" regarding any misconceptions about my role in all of this. If they insisted on keeping me trapped in this hell, then I would own the truth. I have every right to my own life. That included no longer covering for them in the press by saying things like, "They're like family to me. I'm very grateful for the opportunity they gave me." From now on, they could tell their own story and I would most assuredly tell mine.

Later in the same message string, Jerry replied: "You should by now understand that I will not be extorted. I have always treated you fairly and been restrained in response to your threats because I did not wish to ruin your life. Going forward, stop contacting me and my family."

His gaslighting only fueled my desire to set the record straight and salvage my life and reputation. I contacted Aram Roston at Reuters and told him I wanted to go public. There were a number of reporters who I felt had been fair in their articles and sought to convey the complexities of my situation, among them Brandon Ambrosino from Politico, Josh Kovensky at Talking

Points Memo, Michael Miller of the *Washington Post*, and Barnini Chakraborty of Fox News. But Roston had been first, and ultimately I decided to let him be the one to finish it. I didn't need to shop around for a sympathetic mouthpiece because I was telling what really happened, and I had a wealth of corroborating material. I needed a good reporter from a respected organization. Reuters's verification process was so rigorous, even as the powers assembled to fight me were so overwhelming, that we ended up working on it for months.

My narrative and the evidence to back it up were presented to the Falwells in the form of a series of questions, to solicit comment. Their responses were then incorporated into a series of follow-up questions that Roston sent me. Falwell "denies every claim you make, and says your allegations are sensational, uncorroborated, extreme, fantastic, and untruthful" read Roston's missive. They claimed that "what you've told us conflicts with previous public statements you made, and that this means you are not credible." As proof, they presented the 2018 statement that I had prepared.

And there it was—the reason my carefully crafted statement, the one that moved Becki to tell me, "You're an incredible writer!" never appeared in a newspaper. Because it was written as a fallback, to be kept in a bank vault until such time as they needed to tender it for safe passage. Of course it was. What was I thinking?

Moreover, according to the Falwells, I was in an "erratic and untrustworthy psychological and emotional state during the period covered by your [Reuters's] reporting, which was characterized by abusive and racist verbal and physical rages, suicidal states, and a self-destructive pattern of viciously lashing out at those with whom he is close." That I had "a history of explosive, abusive, racist, dishonest, and psychologically problematic behavior directed at hurting those closest to him and self-sabotaging those relationships. Those closest to him have described him as emotionally disturbed, dangerous, vindictive, self-destructive, and suicidal, and further considered having him committed."

But who could have said these awful things about me—much less someone close to me or important in my life? It turns out, according to their letter, "The attorney cites what he says were the Falwells' communications with an ex-girlfriend of yours and quotes her saying of you that 'he had truly unresolved psychological issues that make him hurt people who love him . . . he did the same to his family growing up and now he is doing it to me . . . his snapping and explosive behavior is legitimately scary.' " According to the ex-girlfriend, these comprised "the most fucked up things about my family . . . I have never heard such disgusting racist shit in my life and you can imagine things he said about me too."

This is why Becki reached out to Angelina—and Hailey, and her sisters, and *my* sister—anyone she could get on record at a moment of maximum vulnerability and then save for a rainy day. It's why she spent hours on the phone with me, texting me incessantly, encouraging me to vent, to get it all out so I could feel better. This was the reason I always heard her scribbling on the other end of the line, transcribing our dialogue, furiously trying to get it all down. I thought it was one of her endearing little rituals. Because somehow she always knew this day was coming. Jerry, on Hiltzik's counsel, inducing me to write out their cover story in my own words and Becki gaslighting me into confiding my troubles to her one text at a time were the same thing. These people are survivors. This is what it takes to survive.

I responded to their questions, articulating how they had tried to control me and "control the messaging" for years, volunteered "speaking points," and ultimately reneged on our business deal. After pursuing and controlling me for the better part of a decade, they now portrayed me as an extortionist and a shakedown artist. I reached out to Angelina, who I hadn't been in contact with since our split in 2018. We were not in a good place, but I finally opened up and unburdened myself, explaining to her the true nature of my relationship with the Falwells, and especially Becki. I had kept it all from her, to preserve our own relationship. My intimacy with her and Becki overlapped at the end, and it was something I should have told her about at the time. This was a failure on my part and no one else's. Me. I did this.

Luckily, Angelina was sympathetic to my situation, and incredulous at Becki's duplicity in feigning concern for her, and her utter lack of remorse in weaponizing it to save her own skin. Angelina agreed to speak to Roston and his editors at Reuters, as well as the *Washington Post* and others who ultimately published stories. She also prepared a statement for the *Post*, which we all agreed was to be off the record, so I'll only paraphrase it here. She walked back her statements; explained the background of our emotional breakup; itemized how her comments were often cherry-picked and used out of context; and how she was disgusted at Jerry and Becki's sordid attempts to exploit her emotional vulnerability for their own benefit.

She emphasized the quotes they had selected were sent moments after our breakup. Having now witnessed their duplicity as I had, she could see how my unhealthy relationship with the Falwells and their manipulation of me had generated much of my mental anguish in the first place. My sister also spoke with journalists and confirmed the parts she had witnessed. I am convinced—and deeply grateful—that it was because of their willingness to come forward that the story was ultimately published.

Two weeks before my story went public, in another sign of his hubris, Jerry posted a picture of himself at a party aboard Rick Hendrick's yacht (though Hendrick was not present), for which the whole family flew to Miami. The photo, taken in late July 2020, depicted Jerry with his arm around a young woman, she with her shorts unbuttoned and Jerry with his pants undone, and both sticking out their stomachs. Jerry is holding a cocktail tumbler filled with black liquid. He posted the image on Instagram with the caption, "More vacation shots. Lots of good friends visited us on the yacht. I promise that's just black water in my glass. It was a prop only."

As with so many things associated with Jerry, there was more to the picture than meets the eye. First, the woman, Kathleen Stone, is Becki's assistant. Second, she was pregnant, clearly showing, and had every right to unbutton her Daisy Dukes if she needed. Third, and probably most germane in Jerry's mind, was the fact that they were all in character—hence the "prop" black water. The theme of the party was *Trailer Park Boys*, after a 1999 scatological "mockumentary" set in the eponymous Sunnyvale Trailer Park in Dartmouth, Nova Scotia, which had become a cult hit through seven seasons as a Canadian sitcom, and then in 2013 as an Internet-only series, which soon gravitated to Netflix. It was this last incarnation that had apparently intrigued the

Falwell clan: Jerry was dressed as "Julian," a career criminal (the tell was his blackened beard and ever-present rum and Coke); Becki was "Barb," madam of the Magic Fingers brothel; Trey was the former male prostitute "Randy"; Becki's assistant was "Trinity," the love child of drug dealer "Ricky" (played by Wesley) and porn actress "Lucy" (played by Trey's wife, Sarah), and so on—a genealogy as convoluted as any to be found in the Pentateuch. There was also a video highlight reel from the party of the whole gang in character, but it was taken down once the photo went viral.

And fourth, despite explicit assurances to Kathleen and her husband, Sam, that he would not share the photo with others (as Liberty later alleged in its lawsuit), Jerry posted it anyway for the casual amusement of his 23,000 followers. For me, it carried a particularly unsettling sense memory, as the first time I saw Jerry in private was stretched out on a bed in a Days Inn with his pants undone, leering at me. Now the world knows how I felt.

It wouldn't be the first time the Falwells shared unseemly photos without the subject's permission. Becki's assistant Kathleen is married to Sam Stone, the couple's executive assistant, sometimes referred to as Jerry's "body man," and like Jerry, the son of a famous evangelical preacher—Dave Stone, senior pastor (now retired) of Southeast Christian Church in Louisville, Kentucky, the fourth-largest church in the nation. Both are in the Falwells' inner circle. At Wesley's wedding in 2015, when Becki was miffed I wouldn't sleep with her because I'd brought Angelina with me, she tried to make me jealous by showing me shirtless photos of Sam Stone she had on her phone, similar to the ones I'd seen previously of Ben Crosswhite. In that phone call where she tried to deflect attention away from Ben as someone she was suspiciously close with, Becki also brought up Sam Stone as someone she'd been unfairly linked with.

The response to the yacht photo was immediate and brutal. The photo quickly moved from parody to documentary, blowing a jagged hole in Jerry's carefully constructed public image. The Liberty University community was aghast at the inappropriateness of its president behaving in such a way, and the clear double standard it represented. According to an exhaustively detailed account in a lawsuit filed by Liberty University against Jerry nine months after the event in question, "One online commentator performed an analysis to attempt to gauge the punishment that a Liberty student might endure for posing in this photo, based on the code of conduct in the Liberty Way. The analyst concluded there were 63 counts of potential violation, which would conceivably net a student up to $9,000 in collective financial fines, with a further punishment possible of up to 900 hours of community service." Jerry called into a local radio station to defend himself, succeeding only in drawing additional attention to himself, and noticeably slurring his words during the interview. This is right after Jerry had signed his new, extremely lucrative employment contract and it was becoming clear that their strategy to keep everything contained might not hold.

On August 18, 2020, Reuters received a letter from Jerry's legal and PR firm. Written by Michael Bowe, a partner at Brown Rudnick, it followed up on a phone call of the day before between Roston, two representatives of Reuters, Matthew Hiltzik, Andre Serrano (Jerry's DC-based publicist), and Bowe, which by the tenor of the letter had not gone well. The letter castigates Reuters for not agreeing to accept damaging information "off the record" during the previous day's call (the same play

Hiltzik would later attempt with me and my team), then got down to the business of criticizing their "reporting" (their scare quotes, not mine) "and how utterly untethered your salacious claims were to actual facts. Indeed, you had virtually no basis for 90% of the total story, or 100% of the story as to Jerry Falwell Jr., other than the completely uncorroborated account of your sole source Mr. Granda." And so on for another 2,500 blistering words. "Finally," the letter states in closing, "I remind you that Ms. Becki Falwell is not a public figure and that will not change even if you include her in a false story about her husband."

Like many of the incidental players in this story, Bowe also had a history with Trump. While a litigator with Kasowitz Benson Torres, Bowe and partner Marc E. Kasowitz had two years earlier represented President Trump personally during an FBI investigation into possible collusion between his campaign and the Russian government, a choice that proved awkward in light of Kasowitz's long history with those in Putin's inner circle. These included Russian billionaire industrialist Oleg Deripaska, a longtime client of Paul Manafort; Sberbank, Russia's largest state-owned bank, whose former vice president had recently met with Trump's son-in-law, Jared Kushner, a convergence that was part of the FBI probe; and Trump again in his $5 billion lawsuit against Timothy O'Brien over his 2005 book *Trump-Nation: The Art of Being the Donald*, for claiming that Trump's self-proclaimed worth of between $5 and $6 billion was effectively in the $150 million to $250 million range. Of course, the number of lawyers drawn into Trump's prodigious lawsuits may have quickly exhausted the attorney pool in Washington, DC, connecting everyone to everyone. Still, as I have learned, each of us makes our choices.

Bowe's vehemence in stating Jerry's claims might charitably be attributed to his wanting to please a new client. Specifically, I am told Bowe was hired following further revelations by Politico writer (and Liberty alumnus) Brandon Ambrosino. Ambrosino had first broken the story about Miami Hostel. Two years later, on September 9, 2019, in a Politico story titled, " 'Someone's Gotta Tell the Freakin' Truth': Jerry Falwell's Aides Break Their Silence," he and his coauthors had chronicled how "more than two dozen current and former Liberty University officials describe a culture of fear and self-dealing," which is largely laid at the feet of its current president and chancellor. Jerry responded by alleging a criminal conspiracy involving the board, whose principal crime seems to have been grand theft email. He asked the FBI to investigate, but if they did so, it seems to have been extremely quietly. As of the writing of this book, as far as I know, Bowe continues to represent Jerry in his dealings with Liberty University.

I wanted to make a clean break from Jerry, so I fired Resnick right before I went public. Despite Jerry picking up the tab, my fears of collusion and/or malfeasance did not come to pass; his performance on my behalf remained top-flight. I contemplated hiring a new attorney and filing a civil suit against the Falwells, but to adequately convey the enormity of their transgressions would probably take a book. (To wit.) I also knew that any settlement with them would necessitate a nondisclosure agreement. This time, he would be sure to get it in writing.

The Reuters story ran on August 24, 2020. The day before, Jerry published a 1,200-word Hail Mary column in the *Washington Examiner*, a conservative newsweekly, on his version of the events that had led him here. Making frequent use of scripture—something I had never heard him do once in the seven years I knew him—he acknowledged Becki's short-lived affair with "a former family friend" as "something in which I was not involved," and blames the ensuing stress for having caused him to lose eighty pounds, which made him appear "physically unwell." It was purely in the spirit of forgiveness that they continued their interactions with me following this brief diversion, getting to know my family and loved ones in the process. For this, they were betrayed and extorted, and were now moving to extricate themselves from "this 'fatal attraction' type situation." My spurned response was the impending Reuters feature, devised in cahoots with "a specific member of the media who has continued to badger us," as well as his other media friends. He categorically rejects the "prurient, untrue aspects of this story, however fantastic."

Their game plan from the beginning was for Becki to take the fall, and she accepted that. They had told me this in 2014 when I pressed them on the subject. They figured people would look at me as the wrongdoer, and they would walk away unscathed. Maybe so. Maybe if I had talked about this five years ago, nobody would have believed me. But over the time I had known them, their behavior had become more brazen, entitled, arrogant, and unchecked. I believe once Trump came into the picture that Jerry became drunk on power. But that's only my observation from sitting across the table from him and watching his ambitions take flight. Jerry thought he was bulletproof, and Becki was the Queen of Lynchburg, Our Miss Liberty, and they lived in a bubble of power and privilege that they took with them wherever they went. What do they care what the *New York Times* says? Maybe Becki wouldn't even have to take the fall.

They had me, as ready-made a fall guy as they could ever dream up. Which they probably did. So I did the one thing they never considered I might do. I went public.

"My Dad used to say there's no such thing as bad publicity," Jerry wrote me in a text once, right after that first Aram Roston article in BuzzFeed. "Don't know if he was right or not, but he built the school with 'bad' publicity."

We were about to find out. This was gonna be a new deal for everybody.

CHAPTER 21

WHAT WOULD JESUS DO?

As alleged in the Liberty lawsuit against Jerry, Becki confided in three members of the board that she was concerned about Jerry's drinking, and a plan was put in place for Jerry to step down temporarily and enter a rehab facility, which Liberty would pay for. The board released a statement on August 7, 2020, saying that Jerry would take a leave of absence. Jerry was to remain silent. But by August 17, Jerry was already backsliding—at least in his agreement to enter a treatment facility. Friday, August 21st was the phone call with Roston and his Reuters editor. Saturday the 22nd was the Bowe letter. Sunday the 23rd, Jerry's column ran in the *Examiner*, flouting the gag rule the board had imposed. The Reuters story dropped on Monday, August 24th, and the Liberty board's response was expeditious. By nightfall, Jerry had resigned. For his trouble, he would receive two years' salary as severance and a lump-sum retirement package, which Jerry claimed added up to a grand total of $10.5 million—much of it negotiated against the backdrop of the events depicted in the previous chapters. In a public statement in the *Washington Post*, he tapped that impeccable instinct for both timing and tact: "The quote that keeps running through my mind is Martin Luther King Jr., 'Free at last. Free at last. Thank God almighty, I'm free at last.'"

The day the Reuters story about me came out, Becki texted me, "I hope you're happy and that you were paid well! Jerry just resigned." The same day, she texted Hailey, saying, "I am truly sorry that you are going through this mess. You really seem like a nice girl! Hopefully he has been completely honest with you but I doubt it." Still looking for that chink in the armor, the crack in the wall. The next day, she texted me again: "Lincoln Project," and then, "How much did you get?" That was a little more inscrutable, and it took me a while to figure out what she was getting at.

When the story went public, I got a ton of messages from people I knew, and people I didn't know. Then there was a deluge of media requests. And then—since apparently I wasn't the first one something like this had happened to—a counter-deluge of media professionals offering to help me navigate this onslaught, most of them pro bono. One that stood out to me was Kurt Bardella, a onetime Republican staffer for conservative California congressman Darrell Issa and press secretary for moderate Republican senator Olympia Snowe, who in 2017 left the party over its pandering to the "lunatic fringe." He was also an adviser to the Lincoln Project, a high-profile political action committee founded in the fall of 2019 by moderate business Republicans (i.e., "the party of Lincoln") to combat Trump and his metastasizing control of the party. Kurt helped steer me to the optimal print and broadcast venues, and gave me common-sense advice on how to handle what was altogether a surreal experience.

Jerry chose to interpret this as the Lincoln Project having approached me, paid me off, and sent me out onto the airwaves as a human time bomb. Taking a cue from his pal Trump, he went on the attack, spotlighting his imagined enemies and pandering to the silent majority he imagined as his base rather than choosing to look within, which seems impossible for him. (In the lawsuit he eventually filed against the university on October 28 for defamation and breach of contract, he even roped in Aaron Resnick as a "politically motivated backer" who introduced me to Bardella and a "prominent lawyer in Miami" who financed my expenses, since someone saw me using his credit card. Neither claim is true.)

The Lincoln Project, not having asked to be dragged into this dispute, responded with the following: "The Lincoln Project didn't make Mr. Falwell sit in the corner. The Lincoln Project didn't make Mr. Falwell unbutton his pants on a super yacht and post a picture on social media. The Lincoln Project didn't make Mr. Falwell stand with Donald Trump, though that now makes sense; they are kindred spirits. The Lincoln Project has had nothing to do with the public finally learning about the true character of the Falwell family."

And for the record, I didn't receive a cent for telling my story. My decision to go public was a combination of self-interest and altruism. Jerry and Becki didn't care that I was humiliated by the press after the lawsuit became a matter of public record. And, like the weak man he is, Jerry breached our agreement. Also, I had come to realize he had single-handedly created a toxic culture that systematically abused Liberty University students, faculty, and staff. LU students, parents, employees, and other stakeholders deserved to know who the Falwells were behind their public facade. Several US senators, including both of those from Virginia, have recently demanded a federal investigation into Liberty University, which I support. In addition to the federal investigation, I believe there should be a thorough investigation into the "favors" called in by Michael Cohen on behalf of Donald Trump, and their collusion with the Falwell dynasty. Let's set the record straight with a congressional hearing.

The Aram Roston story and my moment in the media glare would seem to be the capper on my wild roller-coaster ride across the better part of a decade. I said my piece and went back to my life, or what was left of it, and tried to figure out what would happen next. But then, three days after my article ran, in a slowly unfurling story that might be said to feature any number of legitimate bombshells, a piece appeared in Politico by our old friend Brandon Ambrosino that arguably eclipses them all.

According to the article, an unnamed former Liberty student and member of Trey Falwell's band claimed that in 2008 (one year after Jerry Falwell Sr. died), when he was twenty-two, he stayed overnight on the property when band practice ran long. He was sleeping in the converted barn rehearsal space, on the Falwell farm, which the band had nicknamed "House of the Holy" after the 1973 Led Zeppelin album. Sometime in the night, Becki Falwell climbed into bed with him unprovoked and performed oral sex on him. He was a Liberty student at the time.

He used the same term I did to describe Jerry and Becki's on-going behavior—"grooming"—and detailed the efforts to which he had to go to enforce his boundaries—at one point, Becki had called his mom. After rebuffing her further advances, he still had to endure her constant pursuit, Facebook flirtations, and offers of gifts. At one point, she set up a fake Facebook account pretending to be a woman in her twenties using someone else's picture in order to stalk him online. Like me, he backed up his claims with emails, text messages, and screenshots that document, if not the consensual sex, then at least Becki's continuing inappropriate behavior by someone who was a Liberty employee at the time.

The former student claims he only came forward after Becki approached him the week prior, encouraging him to keep their illicit secret. He never filed a complaint with the university, and had told others the story over the years—but like me, also reported struggling with issues of mental health and, in his case, his faith. He also cited Monica Lewinsky, the way she had been treated for coming forward and challenging a presumably great man, and wanted to avoid that altogether. According to the article, Becki texted him on the night Jerry resigned (as she did me), saying, "This is a nightmare. It just keeps getting worse." This strikes me as a degree of self-involvement—seeking solace from your former abuse victim—only achievable by a confirmed narcissist. He responded that he was praying for her. A week later, as reported widely in the press, Jerry got drunk and fell down the stairs in the couple's home, and Becki had to call 911.

On November 1, Ambrosino and two other Politico staff writers, Maggie Severns and Michael Stratford, filed a follow-up story that included corroboration from Becki's neighbor and former confidant, who added that when she cautioned Becki that Jerry would be upset if he found out, Becki told her that the only thing Jerry would be upset about was that he didn't have a chance to watch her have sex with the student. I consider this a validation, given the similarities with my own experience. The Falwells have continued to deny all aspects of the story.

I was once given a collection of reviews Becki had left on the Tripadvisor website, the same as she did for me. There were fourteen separate names by my count, including men, women, and people from seemingly diverse backgrounds. I met two of the women at the Loews Miami Beach, one of whom said they flew her to Lynchburg for potential jobs, and she stayed on the farm with them for a while. I asked Becki about her, and she told me the woman had come on to Jerry and they had to send her home, but I'm not sure that's the most likely explanation.

Throughout the fall of 2020, Becki continued to needle me by text. "How's your girlfriend taking this fame and fortune?! Now you have the money to buy the engagement ring!!!" And again: "You made the cover of *People* magazine. I bet your parents and sister are so proud!"

In the end, I did a ton of print interviews and appeared on *Good Morning America, Anderson Cooper 360,* CNN, and the *NBC Nightly News.* On CNN, I pushed for an independent investigation both publicly and behind the scenes, and Liberty announced such an investigation shortly after my interview. As a personal vindication, I also forced Michael Cohen to recant a version of his story about barking down the pool boy's lawyer, which he told on CNN while pimping his book, having been released in May to serve out his sentence under house arrest over concerns regarding COVID. Most of that week is a blur to me, as the story was playing out in the media and we were both the frequent subjects of cable news sound bites, but I did manage to get hold of a producer at the network and explained why it was impossible that Cohen had spoken to my attorney. Shortly after that call, Cohen corrected himself, claiming he "misspoke," and that he had instead spoken to an attorney for a father and son who had sued Falwell and me over a land deal. CNN issued a correction on their website the next day.

It should be noted that much of what the Falwells gleaned from Angelina—the bulk of the case they make in their Liberty lawsuit—came in the days immediately after Angelina and I had broken up, when Angelina was still in the dark about Becki's true motives and at her most defenseless. It is very much a testament of Angelina's character that she brilliantly tore the Falwells' narrative apart for the benefit of the reporters tasked with vetting this story, which as much as anything I said or did, convinced them of the Falwells' true colors. All of which the lawsuit systematically ignores throughout. "Just stick to the script, 100 percent," like Jerry said going into that first conference call with Aram Roston and the Reuters brain trust.

The lawsuit repeatedly uses the legal phrase "on information and belief," which I had to research: "In the law of evidence, the phrase information and belief identifies a statement that is made, not from firsthand knowledge but 'based on secondhand information that the declarant believes is true.' The phrase is often used in legal pleadings, declarations under penalty of perjury, and affidavits under oath." (This is from *Black's Law Dictionary*.) It is the legal premise for allegations which, when abused, can encompass any wild speculation the plaintiff thinks they can get away with—especially when the plaintiff is grandstanding for show, trying to gin up so much sound and fury. As per *West's Encyclopedia of Law*: This "protects the maker of the statement from claims of outright falsehood or perjury." The phrase is a tell; it reveals the speaker's true intentions.

DARVO is another term I wasn't familiar with, but once I learned it, the whole world snapped into place. It is an acronym for the strategy employed by emotional abusers, credited to author and educator Jennifer Freyd, which stands for "deny, attack, reverse victim and offender" (or "oppressor"). It incorporates what is widely referred to as "gaslighting," and effectively means turning consensus reality inside out so that the perpetrator can now be both victim and hero. As the aggressor begins to believe in their own lies, the technique is designed to disorient the victim, filling them with guilt and shame. I can attest from experience that it feels like a punch to the solar plexus. But once you know the trick, you can see it clearly, and it loses power over you. Attack, never defend. Blame the victim. (Wikipedia uses Donald Trump as a poster child for the term.)

Matt Hiltzik is a trained professional, maybe the best there is, and his clients are under no illusions about the service he provides. They usually get their money's worth. We might roll our eyes at those publicists and media advisers and even crisis managers who get too far out of bounds, who bully and flatter and wheedle and cajole, but it's more or less anticipated. Poisoning the well of civil discourse and doing the work that enables bad people to prolong unspeakable behavior may gain him the admiration of his peers. But it makes the world a nastier, more brutish place.

Jerry's lawsuit was directed at Liberty University and not at me because I don't have any money. The way he sees it, Liberty is respectable and has certain obligations—namely, paying Jerry his money. I'm no lawyer, but I believe this is the reason Liberty took the tack it did in its responding countersuit, filed in April 2021, which was to use the entirety of Jerry's allegations against me—presented without question—as proof that he should have said something about it while he was still president, and particularly before he negotiated an extremely favorable settlement for himself. Even if Liberty mistakenly believed it was still negotiating an employment agreement, and not in effect a severance payout. In its lawsuit, Liberty asked for the return of upward of $40 million. Although Jerry had dropped his initial defamation suit in December 2020, claiming he needed to take a time out, in October 2021, he filed a sixteen-page countersuit to the Liberty suit. The legal wrangling continues as of this writing.

AS FOR MIAMI HOSTEL, IT EVENTUALLY OVERSTAYED ITS WEL-come. What was a good idea at the time eventually saturated and fragmented the local hospitality market, and once the Airbnb market exploded, it was easy to put three bunk beds in all three bedrooms of a luxury condo and appeal to the same clientele on a smaller scale. As with hotels in general, the market evolved and there was no way to compete. But it provided the income stream we were looking for when we needed it, and should have transitioned us into the investment project we always envisioned. Given all that has transpired since then, it's still difficult to see why it didn't.

As it stands, I still hold an equity share in the Alton Hostel, LLC, with two or possibly three business partners I no longer communicate with, save through journalists seeking comment and occasional potshots in the media. From the little I can see over the media transom, my former colleagues don't seem like they're in a good place. There's an independent, feature-length documentary by Billy Corben (*Cocaine Cowboys* and its three sequels) and his producing partner Alfred Spellman, which I have not seen, but in which I and my cowriter Mark Ebner are featured throughout. They tell me it will air on Hulu, but even I know you don't count on anything in the film industry until they've announced the date.

My takeaway on the Falwells is that Becki is very outgoing and charismatic, with a prodigious sexual appetite that she saw no reason she should give up merely because she was a wife, mother, educator, Christian icon, and partisan saint. Jerry enjoys watching her on the hunt and seeing her bag the trophies she brings back to the marital bed, not to mention having his own live-action porn channel at his beck and call. Like a lot of people in his position, he's an aging frat boy addicted to the adrenaline rush of almost getting caught doing things he's not supposed to, whether it's sharing illicit photos, making off-color jokes, saying the quiet part out loud, using a corporate jet for personal vacations, treating the university as his on-call ATM or to reward friends, family, and furtive conquests, turning his wife out like the Whore of Babylon, or flouting the fundamental tenets of Christianity. All of this is backstopped by his privilege, influence, and family legacy, which he has managed to systematically squander in record time.

Jerry has an estimated war chest of $100 million. That will build him his own big, beautiful wall between whatever lifestyle he and his family settle on and the outside world that might pass judgment on it. People like that rarely pay for their crimes, they just move the borders of their empire closer and closer to home, where they might oversee their dominion from the front porch, say, a glass of "black water" always within reach from their favorite chair.

The sex was never the issue; it was the hypocrisy and the abuse of power. Because they helm an institution whose business it is to shame others for what they do in private, and to hold the threat of shame over them to demand fealty and subservience.

I have my story to tell, along with whatever means I have to back it up. But there are all the untold stories as well: the ones harvested by Save71, a group of current and former Liberty students advocating new leadership and meaningful change, or from the many journalists working the story I've become friendly with, to Christian academics like Karen Swallow Prior or Marybeth Baggett who would like for Christianity to survive the profiteers and tent show revivalists that coalesced around the evangelical movement of the late seventies and got high on the top-fuel fumes of power and political influence. (I may disagree with Prior's position opposing abortion, but she has been a tireless supporter of the Jane Does, and she sounded an early alarm on the corrosive effect of Trump-like politics on the Liberty ecosystem.) And the women—the dozen-plus survivors of rape and sexual abuse who have banded together in a multi-plaintiff lawsuit against the university for facilitating a culture where female students were reduced to prey—and the many more chronicled on the periphery of that group, in the *Gangster Capitalism* podcast and many, many publications, whose stories are uniformly harrowing. There are quite possibly hundreds more victims out there, some of whom have found their way to me directly, as some kind of bellwether of a phenomenon I had no clue about, and for whom my decision to go public dislodged something in the ether, in ways I could have never imagined. Measured against their stories, my own journey pales in comparison.

I've tried to follow the many tangled leads that continue to come my way and braid them into the emerging whole, but much of this is better left in the hands of experts. Whatever precipice I've wound up at, I urge those with the skills and tenacity to keep digging for the truth.

This is a story where, despite it dominating my life for the past decade, we've still only scratched the surface. I can say with confidence that if this had never happened to me, if I had seen the future coming like I should have, and followed a more traditional path, I would be much further along right now in every way.

But this is the life I have, so I plan to make the best of it. And there is a generation of Liberty graduates and evangelical true believers who are slowly coming out of their deep freeze, who realize they've been lied to by their politicians, their religious leaders, and their own hopes and dreams. They want this story told as much as I do. I'm ready to take my life and my story back, and to put it out there in the world.

THE LIBERTY WAY

Eight months after Jerry resigned, in late April 2021, he and Becki posted a video online announcing they would be hosting a party at their farm for graduating seniors and their dates. Between the raft of bad publicity the Falwells had visited on the university, and the dueling lawsuits that had both sides hyperventilating in their escalating claims against each other, Lynchburg's former First Couple had been personae non grata on the campus they once reigned over. It appeared that the old Jerry and Becki were making a comeback. But not everyone embraced the idea.

Chelsea Andrews, the 2015 Liberty senior class president and an alumni-activist, launched a petition against the party, signed by seventy-one of her fellow alumni and a few current students, on the grounds that accused sexual predators had no business welcoming underage students into their home. A family home, as she put it in a companion letter to the Liberty Board, "where his wife is alleged to have initiated oral sex on a drunk, sleeping student." In that same letter, she expressed concern over recent rumors that a long-awaited independent investigation—the so-called Baker Tilley report, conducted by an independent accounting firm—would focus solely on financial impropriety rather than sexual violations. That is, Liberty would make sure they got their money, and had taken decisive measures to ensure that, while the growing number of victims of sexual assault on the Liberty campus—and on Jerry Falwell's watch as president and chancellor—would receive no such satisfaction.

The letter called for an alumni advisory board or board of directors, to include both women and persons of color, as an antidote to Jerry's racist comments and the couple's predatory behavior, and that such behavior be investigated, transparently and in all due haste, using all of the university's available resources. To encourage them in this endeavor, Chelsea posted the letter to Twitter, where I saw it, along with the rest of the Liberty universe. I immediately sent her a private message:

Hi Chelsea,

I want to let you know that I'm proud of you for speaking up against abuse of power, corruption, and predatory behavior. After going public about the Falwells, I gained many allies who share a mutual goal—holding the Falwells and the Board accountable.

Let me know if you want to talk (off the record—anonymous).

Chelsea responded to my message, which began a dialogue between us. I was to learn that the issue of sexual assault was not a casual one for her. She said that in 2014, as a student at Liberty, she had been assaulted by a former student leader. Then in August, three months after her assault, Chelsea was raped by a graduate medical student, as she alleges in her subsequent complaint as Jane Doe #7. She was a virgin, and had been the National Day of Purity chairperson the semester before, extolling the virtues of chastity. (All personal details of Chelsea's story are printed here with her consent.) A fast-rising star in campus government and by extension the conservative political firmament, she immediately grasped that bringing this to the attention of the administration would also open her to violations of the storied Liberty Way, thus possibly impeding her path to a promising career, and decided not to report the incident. In 2021, she was starting to process her rape, which she had only discussed in vague, qualified terms. The act of launching a petition on the topic inspired several women with similar stories to contact her privately. So, she put her story down in a letter to Liberty general counsel David Corry, and alerted him there were others like herself, and they wished to be heard. According to Chelsea, he never responded. However, a day later, Jerry canceled the party, allegedly for health reasons. (He had "respiratory emboli symptoms"—tiny blood clots in his lungs.)

The Falwells' involvement with campus life has been strictly monitored since. In order to see their daughter, Caroline, graduate in 2022, for instance, they had to agree to walk directly from their car to their seats, take no photographs on the property (selfies included), leave as soon as the ceremony was over, and speak to no one. Meanwhile, Jonathan Falwell, Jerry's brother and pastor of Thomas Road Baptist Church, has quietly replaced

David Nasser as campus pastor, in a move many see as a preliminary step to ease him into the role of chancellor, now cleaved
from the presidency, to assure a line of succession inside the chosen family.

Over time, Chelsea and I became friends of sorts, bound
by a common cause. She credits me with the timing of her going public with her assault, despite the fact that there is a two-
year statute of limitations on assault in Virginia, which she and
others are working to get changed. Eventually, a dozen women
came forward (their number ultimately swelled to twenty-two)
to tell gruesome stories of campus assaults, but also of an administration that seemed hidebound in discouraging them from
speaking out, equally intimidating in their response and unsym-
pathetic to their emotional plight. In 2021, the women hired a
lawyer and filed a multi-plaintiff lawsuit against the university
under Title IX of the Education Amendments of 1972, which
prohibits sex-based discrimination for colleges that receive federal funding, and specifically the Clery Act, which, as amended
in 2013 (quoting from Liberty's website) "requires higher education institutions to annually report certain information con-
cerning campus security policies and campus crime statistics."
They are known as the "Jane Does" for their anonymous appearance in court documents.

The saga of alleged sexual assault victims at Liberty was
chronicled by reporter Hannah Dreyfus in ProPublica on October 24, 2021, and her account is grueling: evidence was ignored;
photos of bruises and physical evidence went missing from victims' files; police discouraged victims from filing charges or they
weren't made aware that was an option. Witnesses' statements
were twisted to claim the opposite of their intention; the coun-

seling center turned victims away when "they didn't have any appointments available"; victims failed to come forward on the strength of these implicit threats; assailants faced no disciplinary actions; and women who frequently encountered their attackers on campus stopped going to class. The university's unique focus on sexual purity—in the form of "victim notices" they must sign acknowledging the possibility of disciplinary action for violating the Liberty Way—was also used as a cudgel to dissuade victims from pursuing formal action. Scott Lamb, Liberty's senior vice president of communications, responded to the allegations less than a month after he was fired, he claims, due to his whistleblowing on Liberty's handling of Title IX sexual misconduct accusations. He termed Liberty's response "a conspiracy of silence."

My coauthor and I spoke with a number of the sexual assault victims who came forward—those in the Jane Doe lawsuit and others who were too late to qualify. Those who are quoted here gave their permission. Jane Doe #16 alleges she was sexually assaulted by a current member of Liberty's football team. Afterward, she went to the emergency room, and the next day to the Title IX office on the Liberty campus. Through the Title IX process, she says, her assailant was cleared of all liability—both initially and on appeal. Two days after she filed her complaint, another student filed an almost identical complaint against the same player, and in his statement, he conflated details of the two victims. Under the username "thelastjanedoe," she later posted on Instagram, "My assailant is playing on the Liberty football field. Right. Now. And he shouldn't be. He is responsible for rape, assault, and trauma. I have been fighting my hardest for months and months, and I'm not going to stop now." After repeatedly running into her attacker on campus, she unenrolled in May of 2022.

The player in question was recruited during the tenure of Hugh Freeze, the former head football coach at the University of Mississippi, and before that a legendary Memphis high school coach profiled in the book *The Blind Side*, by Michael Lewis, and the movie of the same name. During his five years at Ole Miss, from 2012 to 2017, twenty-seven of Freeze's thirty-nine wins were ultimately vacated for recruitment and academic standards violations, with Freeze himself forced to resign after it was discovered he had placed a dozen calls to a Tampa-based escort service on a university cell phone. Not long after, Jerry spearheaded a move to hire him as head coach of the Liberty Flames. He reportedly flew down and closed the deal personally, which came with a $3 million salary (considered a bargain) and a house built especially for him atop a mountain overlooking the campus.

This was followed by hiring athletic director Ian McCaw, after he'd resigned from the Baylor University coaching staff amid multiple sexual assault charges against the Baylor Bears football team, a scandal that eventually saw the resignation of Chancellor Kenneth Starr. Some might argue this is just good business sense, picking up proven talent at bargain prices. But it also has the added effect of surrounding Jerry with the survivors of sex scandals, creating a culture that accepts and protects those guilty of abuse of power, corruption, and predatory behavior. Football remains the largest source of income for Liberty outside of online enrollment.

Keith Anderson, a former dean of students and current executive director of health and wellness, is accused of sexual predation by both Jane Doe #1 and Jane Doe #8 in the Does' lawsuit.

Both were employees; Jane Doe #1 claims he showed up in the middle of the night and forced his way into her apartment, made her take what he claimed was allergy medication, and that she woke up with his hands on her neck. She alleges that he later threatened to have her deported, and she was ultimately fired. Jane Doe #8 says he sexually harassed her and created a toxic working environment, soon forcing her to quit. Anderson is also a preacher at a small local church. As the producer of *Gangster Capitalism*, which included both women's stories in its podcast, asked in a tweet: "Why does he still have a job?" (Anderson failed to respond to repeated requests for comment.)

Chelsea and the others are part of a robust community of survivors that now find compassion in each other, the one thing the university was tasked with and failed to provide. She became part of the lawsuit as Jane Doe #7, appeared on *Gangster Capitalism*, a podcast that drew national attention to this issue and provided numerous harrowing details—both of the crimes themselves and insensitivity on the part of the university. In early May 2022, many of the Jane Does settled with the university for undisclosed amounts. This was just as the Southern Baptist Convention, which includes all southern evangelical Baptist churches, released a scathing report detailing rampant sexual abuses within the church hierarchy, extending to some of the most esteemed figures in the denomination, which had effectively been covered up going back twenty years. The SBC report has been widely compared to the Spotlight investigations of the Roman Catholic Church's Boston archdiocese in 2003, which revealed similar systemic failures and widespread cover-up, with at least one observer calling the current revelations "an apocalypse."

One of those who didn't settle was Jane Doe #15. The subject of a special bonus episode of *Gangster Capitalism*, her alleged assault was perhaps the most brutal of those recounted; she claims she was gang-raped in 2001 by five men in a Lynchburg shopping mall as an eighteen-year-old Liberty student, became pregnant as a result and was stalked on campus by one of her assailants with a knife, only to then be threatened with disciplinary action by the university. As an alternative, she says, she was advised by a dean that if she entered a residential program for unmarried mothers, the Liberty Godparent Home, and agreed to give up her baby, she would receive a free four-year scholarship.

Jane Doe #15 states that although cases of her severity would normally merit a settlement of between $2 million and $5 million, Liberty's opening offer was $5,000, and their final offer was $35,000, citing the statute of limitations of only two years, which made it impossible for them to pursue their case in civil court. She claims she found their offer "insulting." (In response to a list of questions about Jane Doe #15 and other Jane Does, a Liberty spokesperson sent my coauthor a set of previously issued press releases, none of which specifically addressed their claims.)

Representatives of the Department of Education recently conducted over seventy interviews at Liberty, where they are investigating the university for potential violations of the Clery Act. Meanwhile, new Title IX recommendations are reportedly coming from the Biden administration by way of an executive order. And Tom Arnold is producing a documentary series to focus on several of the women at the center of the lawsuit. Chelsea will be among the participants.

But why would the Liberty administration go to such lengths

to put their own students in harm's way, in contravention of established law and simple decency? If there are sexual predators operating within Liberty's confines, why not root them out and punish them?

In his lawsuit against Liberty, to establish his bona fides, Jerry and his lawyers included the following paragraph: "Under Mr. Falwell's stewardship, Liberty University's stature increased exponentially by almost every metric, especially enrollment and financials. Between just 2007 and 2020 alone, attendance increased from 9,600 students in residence and 27,000 students online to 15,000 students in residence and 108,000 students studying online. And, after decades of financial hardship, Liberty now boasts a $1.6 billion endowment—one of the nation's largest. More students enrolled and more donors gave because of Mr. Falwell's tireless efforts in carrying out his father's vision for Liberty."

Although Jerry is widely credited with turning around the university's financial prospects, the $100 million debt that was racked up by his father was largely retired by a $70 million donation from insurance magnate Art Williams—Mark DeMoss's father-in-law. (The same Mark DeMoss who resigned from Liberty's board.) Arthur DeMoss, Mark's father, was also a generous patron of the university, as was Reverend Sun Myung Moon and his Unification Church, through his relationship with Falwell Sr. crony Ron Godwin (who Jerry also showed the door). Jerry's agency in Liberty's financial resurrection was sealed by his father's claims in his 1997 autobiography, which could have been to shore up the line of succession as much as anything else. When the elder Falwell died unexpectedly a decade later, Liberty was the beneficiary of his $34 million life insurance policy (some of the money went to Thomas Road Baptist Church), rendering the university officially debt-free. A similar but lesser-known bequest from his wife, Macel, in 2015, of unknown but comparable value, was also directed to Liberty.

Liberty's most prominent donations came in large part from immensely wealthy, extremely conservative businessmen who liked the political philosophy that Liberty espoused and wished to see it proliferate. And Liberty was able to keep its faculty on message mainly by refusing to grant tenure, as a means of controlling the message. This may have represented a profound marketing tool in attracting conservative Christian parents with fears for their children loose in a secular world, but it was a death sentence for Liberty's reputation as a repository of higher learning. Some reputable academics avoided it outright; others, like Karen Swallow Prior, eventually resigned (after her "release time" to speak and write was canceled and, as she explains, her "Never Trump" stance made her resignation a foregone con-clusion). There is no real curriculum, no medical degrees save for a doctor of osteopathy degree. The one course that anyone mentions is called Apologetics—Jerry took it as an undergrad—which teaches the art of defending the Christian faith when its believers are set upon by infidels and apostates, a kind of rhetori-cal jujitsu to get you out of any philosophical throwdown.

To this mix, Jerry had the brilliant idea of expanding the school's presence online, increasing their enrollment from just under 40,000 in 2007 when he took over as president to roughly 110,000 today, 15,000 of whom attend the main campus. According to the *Chronicle of Higher Education*, that represents the second-highest online enrollment in the country, surpassed only by the University of Phoenix. ProPublica reports that in

2017, Liberty students received $772 million in federal grants ($100 million of it in Pell grants for low-income students), and roughly 85 percent of undergraduates receive some form of financial assistance, with a median debt of $25,000 after graduation (as reported by Politico). In the words of Dustin Wahl, who founded an organization called Save71 in the wake of revelations about the Falwells and Liberty, the campus is "a small nonprofit that runs a gigantic for-profit college." No wonder Jerry hates Title IX so much. Were the current violations to compromise Liberty's tax-exempt status, it would amount to a reckoning Liberty could scarce survive.

As we were preparing this book for publication—April 28, 2022—a story dropped in the *New Yorker* titled "Can Liberty University Be Saved?" Written by veteran journalist Megan K. Stack, it chronicled Jerry Falwell's fall from grace and attempted salvation. Most of the story was given over to Dustin Wahl and his Save71 group, and coming to terms with Liberty in the post-Falwell era. I spoke with the author and am quoted briefly, preferring at this late stage to largely keep my own counsel, saving my remaining recollections for this book and companion documentary. But I found her reporting thorough and observations astute.

What leaped out of the story, though, was that after visiting the Falwell farm last spring—the same pilgrimage, replete with bucolic imagery and golden-hour photography, made by writer Gabriel Sherman for his *Vanity Fair* profile—she spoke with them again ten months later. In the interim, she had obviously read Sherman's piece, and she asked about the charges of sexual assault Becki had leveled at me, which had not been part of her previous reporting. On speakerphone, Jerry admitted—

well, here, I'll let Stack tell it: "They were preoccupied with the tell-all book and documentary expected from Granda in coming months, and Falwell said they'd thought that perhaps news of his wife's sexual-assault allegation might 'kill his book.' 'I wanted us to be able to tell the story first,' he said. 'I know, when he tells it, it's gonna be full of lies.'" In an in-house interview on the *New Yorker* website, Stack reflected on the remark, and by extension on Jerry as an improbable character, cloven with contradictions: "I thought that was a strange thing to tell me," she says. "Even if that's true, why would you say it? So, there were these moments when they would say exactly what they wanted to say, seemingly to their own detriment. They were some of the most interesting subjects that I've talked to in my career."

In the *New Yorker* story, author and theology professor David Baggett, who along with his wife, Marybeth Baggett, were among the shrinking number of reputable academics at Liberty, and who finally left last year, is quoted as saying that certain "pockets of the evangelical world today," and Falwell in particular, rely on God's grace to pass directly from sin to redemption. And yet "there's this intermediary step according to Christian theology—which is repentance."

"Jerry Falwell Jr. has asked for forgiveness," writes Stack, "but he has never, to my knowledge, apologized for his behavior. He is not sorry for anything . . ."

And there was another thing that came out of that *Vanity Fair* feature, which I only found out about recently. After the story ran in the March issue, Chelsea received an out-of-nowhere text from Becki. They had crossed paths at Liberty, given Chelsea's extensive extracurricular activities, including something called Ladies of Liberty her sophomore year, in which she organized a slumber party for the wives of pastors and campus dignitaries in the Hancock Welcome Center (and at which Becki pulled out lingerie, which was awkward at the time). Becki also once wrote her a letter of recommendation. Sent on March 21 at 9:16 p.m., the text reads in total, "This is Becki. Is this Chelsea?" Chelsea didn't respond, on the advice of her attorney. Chelsea assumes she was trying to do damage control, or just trying to get intel.

According to those who worked with him in communications, Scott Lamb had initially been hired to cowrite Jerry's autobiography. The author of several books, including *Huckabee: The Authorized Biography* and *The Faith of Donald J. Trump: A Spiritual Biography*, cowritten with David Brody, Lamb claimed at one point to have been the second-highest-paid employee of the university. In March 2019, Tobi Laukaitis, a journalism major working in news writing, social media, and public relations, remembers IT head John Gauger showing up to oversee half their operations, and to help Jerry build a website. Her team had the distinct impression that Jerry was considering a run for office. But Lamb's fortunes changed when the Jane Doe lawsuit fell into his in-basket and he had to start defending an indefensible and intractable position to an increasingly less credulous press corps.

"The problem isn't the PR," Lamb says memorably in the ProPublica article. "The problem is the problem." Lamb is one of the few with the university who stood up for what's right, and the university is suing him for up to $3 million for defamation. He's also been ordered to turn over all official documents in his possession as "trade secrets." As of this writing, his claims against Liberty have been dismissed, and he has moved to re-plead his allegations. Whatever happens to Lamb, at least he's on the right side of history.

Go walk the pristine grounds of Liberty University today; everywhere you look the legacy of the most famous Falwell scion, and his memory, is invisible. It has been dismantled and buried as thoroughly as the statues of the Confederate dead. He is not mentioned in the standard speech a new generation of bushy-tailed acolytes deliver to visitors or incoming classes, and he has been sandblasted from the website as systematically as Mark De-Moss once was from the building that bore his family name. The board, or at least its executive committee, turned his own defense against him, used the fiction he made of me to once again absolve him of blame as a battering ram to pummel him into submission. Once everyone sobers up, and considers what happened in the pale light of a new day, they'll see that they were in agreement all along: nobody wants a showdown in court. Messy court trials are fought with depositions, and depositions reveal secrets, and nobody wants that. Both sides will walk it back and arrive at a number, known only to them, and that will be that. A true accounting is beyond the scope of anyone's better angels.

Jerry confided to me once that he thought a new civil war was imminent. That was the appeal of Trump; he allowed weak, pampered men like Jerry to dress up as wartime dandies, sporting plumes and epaulettes and the respect of the men who serve under him, confident in the knowledge that his chosen legacy would survive him, burnished and glowing in a stolen light. So, who knows? Trump is planning his return in 2024, there's always a place for the faithful; they can get the old gang back together. It'll be just like old times.

I last heard from Jerry through my writing partner. He referred to me as a cautionary tale, saying, "He's going to find himself sitting in prison . . ." We'll see.

Beyond the Jane Does and their silent contingent, as well

as anyone else who ever got in the Falwells' way and bore the brunt of their undiluted anger, the real victims are the students of Liberty, and beyond them, true believers in organized religion, who take seriously the teachings they came there to study. Over the course of my many visits to Liberty, I went from seeing the students and staff there as blind adherents, even members of an invisible cult, to those whose spiritual beliefs are ever-present in their lives. Many of them I have enduring respect for: people like Karen Swallow Prior, a principled scholar who was banished for the sin of independence. Dustin Wahl, the best and brightest his generation has to offer, whose exposure to Jerry Falwell Jr. and his petty exercise of power manifested a course correction inside of him. Or Chelsea Andrews, a warrior who bears her battle scars as openly and proudly as any returning veteran, and lives with a deep spiritual purpose.

They didn't deserve for this innate longing to be exploited by charlatans, wolves in expensive wool jackets. Either Jerry and his ilk, who see it as a vessel for personal glory; or his brother, Jonathan, who as far as I can tell is just Jerry minus the hedonism and sense of humor, but with the same glowering suspicion of those outside of his control; or even old man Falwell, a barnstormer and carnival barker at heart, the son of bootleggers, marginalized in his own time, who saw the erosion of the separation of church and state as a means to earthly power and secular reward. Maybe that was his own temptation in the desert; if so, he failed miserably. And certainly, a board of directors who would preside over all of this with a blind eye and feigned beneficence. All of them will face their own reckoning soon enough, just as soon as the curtains 'round them fall. Religion has been a force for good in the world, and it could be once again. Instead, it lies in shards. Here's hoping a next generation can pick up the pieces.

ACKNOWLEDGMENTS

Gratitude goes to Murray Weiss, Joel Gotler, and James Sammataro for the astute agenting and counsel that landed us with top-notch editor Mauro DiPreta and his outstanding team at William Morrow.

My story could not have been told without the inimitable Tom Arnold, Dustin Wahl of Save71—and Billy Corben, Alfred Spellman, David Cypkin, and Nicole Pritchett at Rakontur Films.

Inspiration came from many—especially Zak Levitt, Andrew Jenks, and the *Gangster Capitalism* podcast crew, esteemed scholars Marybeth Baggett and Karen Swallow Prior, and all the courageous Liberty University Jane Does I've been honored to cross paths with.

Unsung in all this are my family and close friends in Miami and DC for their love and support, and those who have been supporting me publicly and behind the scenes.

Mark Ebner thanks Paul Cullum and rock star transcriber Sylvia Juncosa—without whom, collaborations as good as this one do not happen.